The History of Beer

Crafted by Skriuwer

Copyright © 2024 by Skriuwer.

All rights reserved. No part of this book may be used or reproduced in any form whatsoever without written permission except in the case of brief quotations in critical articles or reviews.

For more information, contact : **kontakt@skriuwer.com** (www.skriuwer.com)

Table of Contents

1. Introduction to Beer
1.1 The Origins of Beer: A Global Perspective
1.2 The Earliest Evidence: Mesopotamia and Egypt
1.3 The Social Role of Beer in Early Civilizations
1.4 The Ingredients: Barley, Water, and Yeast
1.5 How Beer Spread Across Continents

2. Beer in Ancient Civilizations
2.1 Beer in Mesopotamian Culture: The Sumerians and Babylonians
2.2 The Role of Beer in Ancient Egyptian Society
2.3 Beer and Rituals: Religious and Ceremonial Use in Ancient Cultures
2.4 The Discovery of Fermentation: Scientific and Cultural Impact
2.5 Beer in Early European Societies: The Celts and Germanic Tribes

3. Beer in the Middle Ages
3.1 Monks and Brewing: The Role of Monasteries in Beer Production
3.2 The Influence of Religion: Brewing in Christian and Islamic Cultures
3.3 The Development of Hops: A Key Ingredient in Beer
3.4 Beer and Daily Life in Medieval Europe
3.5 The Rise of Brewing Guilds and Regulations

4. Beer in the Renaissance and Enlightenment
4.1 The Rise of Commercial Breweries: Beer as an Industry
4.2 Scientific Discoveries: Louis Pasteur and the Pasteurization of Beer
4.3 The Cultural Role of Beer in European Society
4.4 Beer and Trade: The Influence of Global Commerce
4.5 Brewing Technology Innovations: From Barrels to Bottles

5. Beer and the Industrial Revolution
5.1 The Impact of the Industrial Revolution on Brewing Processes
5.2 The Emergence of Lager: A New Type of Beer
5.3 Mass Production and the Growth of Global Beer Brands
5.4 The Role of Immigration in Beer's Spread: German Brewers in America
5.5 Beer in the Age of Railroads: Transportation and Distribution

6. Beer in Colonial America
6.1 Beer in Early Settlements: Jamestown and Plymouth
6.2 The Role of Beer in American Revolution
6.3 Beer vs. Cider: Popular Drinks in Colonial Times
6.4 Brewing in the New World: The Challenges of New Ingredients
6.5 The First American Breweries: Foundations of a Brewing Nation

7. Beer and Prohibition
7.1 The Temperance Movement: Early Calls for Prohibition
7.2 Prohibition in the United States: 1920–1933
7.3 The Impact of Prohibition on the Beer Industry
7.4 Bootlegging and Speakeasies: Beer in the Underground Market
7.5 The Repeal of Prohibition: The Return of Legal Beer

8. The Globalization of Beer
8.1 The Expansion of Beer into Asia and Africa
8.2 European Beer Traditions in the Americas
8.3 The Growth of Multinational Brewing Corporations
8.4 Beer Tourism: Festivals, Breweries, and Tasting Events
8.5 Beer and Global Trade: Exporting Beer Across Continents

9. Beer and Politics
9.1 Beer Taxes: Historical and Modern Examples
9.2 Beer as a Political Tool: Public Houses and Revolutions
9.3 The Impact of War on Beer Production and Consumption
9.4 Government Regulation of Beer in Different Countries
9.5 Beer and Diplomacy: How Beer Is Used in International Relations

10. The Rise of Craft Beer
10.1 The Craft Beer Revolution: Origins in the Late 20th Century
10.2 Microbreweries and Brewpubs: A New Way of Brewing
10.3 The Role of Craft Beer in Local Economies
10.4 Beer Styles in the Craft Movement: IPAs, Stouts, and Sours
10.5 Craft Beer Festivals and Tasting Events

11. Beer and Health
11.1 The Historical Belief in Beer as Medicine
11.2 The Nutritional Value of Beer: Myths and Facts
11.3 The Impact of Beer on Public Health
11.4 Beer and the "Beer Belly": Separating Fact from Fiction
11.5 Responsible Drinking: Moderation and Enjoyment

12. Beer and Art
12.1 Beer in Literature: From Ancient Poems to Modern Novels
12.2 The Role of Beer in Visual Art: Paintings, Advertisements, and Branding
12.3 Beer in Music: Songs, Ballads, and Pub Culture
12.4 The Aesthetic of Beer: Labels, Logos, and Packaging
12.5 Beer and Festivals: Oktoberfest and Other Beer Celebrations

13. Beer in Modern Popular Culture
13.1 Beer in Film and Television: Iconic Moments
13.2 Beer and Sports: The Relationship Between Beer Brands and Sporting Events
13.3 The Rise of Beer Influencers on Social Media
13.4 Beer Challenges and Trends: Viral Challenges and Beer Consumption
13.5 The Role of Advertising in Shaping Beer Culture

14. The Science of Brewing
14.1 The Chemistry Behind Beer: Fermentation, Yeast, and Sugars
14.2 How Water Chemistry Affects Beer Styles
14.3 Innovations in Brewing Technology: Automated Brewing Systems
14.4 Yeast Strains and Their Influence on Flavor
14.5 Sustainable Brewing: Eco-Friendly Practices in the Beer Industry

15. Beer and Gastronomy
15.1 The Art of Beer Pairing: Complementing Food with Beer
15.2 Cooking with Beer: Traditional and Modern Recipes
15.3 Beer and Cheese Pairing: A Guide for Enthusiasts
15.4 Beer Dinners: Multi-Course Meals with Beer Pairings
15.5 The Role of Beer in Fine Dining: How Top Chefs Use Beer in Menus

16. The Future of Beer
16.1 The Impact of Climate Change on Beer Production
16.2 Technological Innovations in Brewing: The Use of AI
16.3 The Growth of Non-Alcoholic Beer
16.4 Sustainability in Beer Production: Reducing Water and Energy Usage
16.5 New Frontiers: Experimentation with Ingredients and Styles

17. Beer Around the World
17.1 German Beer Culture: Reinheitsgebot and Traditions
17.2 Belgian Beer: Abbeys, Trappists, and Lambics
17.3 The British Pub: Ale, Bitter, and the Role of Beer in British Society
17.4 American Craft Beer: The Evolution of a New Tradition
17.5 Beer in Asia: The Rise of Craft Breweries in China and Japan

18. Beer and Gender
18.1 Women and Beer: From Ancient Brewsters to Modern Brewers
18.2 Gendered Marketing in the Beer Industry: Breaking Stereotypes
18.3 The Rise of Women-Led Breweries and Craft Beer Brands
18.4 The History of Beer as a Gender-Neutral Drink
18.5 Women in Beer Festivals and Competitions

19. Beer and Sustainability
19.1 Reducing Waste in Brewing: Eco-Friendly Practices
19.2 The Rise of Organic and Biodynamic Beer
19.3 Water Conservation in Brewing: A Growing Concern
19.4 Recycling Spent Grains: Innovations in Reusing Byproducts
19.5 Solar-Powered Breweries: Green Energy in Brewing

20. The Role of Beer in Modern Society
20.1 Beer as a Social Lubricant: The Role of Beer in Social Gatherings
20.2 Beer and Identity: Craft Beer Enthusiasts and the Rise of Beer Communities
20.3 Beer and the Economy: Its Contribution to Employment and GDP
20.4 The Role of Beer in Celebrations: Weddings, Holidays, and Special Occasions
20.5 Beer and Social Change: Charity and Philanthropy in the Beer Industry

Chapter 1

Introduction to Beer

The Origins of Beer: A Global Perspective

Beer, one of humanity's oldest fermented beverages, boasts a history that spans millennia and cultures, reflecting the diverse culinary traditions and social practices of societies around the world. Its origins can be traced back to various ancient civilizations, each contributing unique ingredients and methods that laid the groundwork for the breweries of today.

The earliest evidence of beer production dates back to around 7000–6000 BCE in ancient China, where archaeological findings suggest that fermented beverages made from rice, honey, and fruit were created. This early form of beer highlights the fundamental human instinct to ferment and create enjoyable drinks from available resources. However, it is in the fertile region of Mesopotamia, particularly in Sumer (modern-day Iraq), where beer took on a more recognizable form. The Sumerians are credited with one of the earliest documented recipes for beer, found in the "Hymn to Ninkasi," a goddess associated with brewing, dating back to around 1800 BCE. This hymn describes the brewing process and ingredients, including barley and emmer wheat, underscoring the importance of beer in Sumerian culture.

In ancient Egypt, beer played a central role in daily life and was consumed by people of all social classes. It was a staple part of the diet, often safer to drink than water due to the fermentation process that killed harmful pathogens. Egyptians brewed various types of beer using barley, which was a key crop in the region. Beer was also integral to religious rituals, with offerings made to deities and used in funerary practices. The significance of beer in these ancient societies illustrates its role not just as a beverage but as a cultural artifact that shaped social structures and customs.

As civilizations advanced, so too did the methods of brewing and the global spread of beer. The introduction of hops in brewing, which began in the 9th century in Europe, transformed beer's flavor profile and preservation methods. This innovation coincided with the rise of monasteries in medieval Europe, where monks refined brewing techniques, leading to the establishment of brewing as an organized craft. Monasteries became centers of brewing excellence, producing quality beer that was often traded or consumed during religious festivities.

The globalization of beer truly accelerated during the Age of Exploration in the 15th and 16th centuries. European colonizers and traders introduced beer to the Americas, Africa, and Asia, where local ingredients and brewing traditions began to merge with European styles. In North America, early settlers brewed beer using indigenous grains and techniques, setting the stage for a flourishing beer culture that would evolve into the craft beer movement of the late 20th century.

In each region, beer took on unique characteristics. For example, in Belgium, the tradition of brewing lambics and Trappist ales emerged, while in Germany, the purity law, Reinheitsgebot, established strict standards for beer production using only water, barley, and hops. These regional distinctions contributed to a rich tapestry of beer styles that are celebrated worldwide today.

In summary, the origins of beer illustrate a fascinating journey through time and across cultures. From ancient China and Mesopotamia to the modern craft breweries of today, beer has not only survived but thrived, adapting to the tastes and traditions of each society it touches. As a beverage that bridges social divides, beer continues to play a vital role in human culture, serving as a symbol of creativity, community, and celebration across the globe.

The Earliest Evidence: Mesopotamia and Egypt

The history of beer can be traced back over 7,000 years, with some of the earliest evidence originating from the ancient civilizations of Mesopotamia and Egypt. These regions not only provide the earliest documented instances of beer production but also highlight the drink's integral role in social, economic, and religious practices of early human societies.

In Mesopotamia, particularly in the Sumerian city-states such as Uruk and Eridu, archaeological findings reveal that beer was a staple in the daily diet. The Sumerians are credited with the earliest known recipe for beer, found on a cuneiform tablet dating back to around 1800 BCE. This tablet, known as the Hymn to Ninkasi, is both a prayer to the goddess of beer and a detailed recipe for brewing, showcasing the significance of beer in their culture. The ingredients listed include barley, water, and a type of bread called bappir, which acted as a fermentation starter. This early form of beer was likely a thick, porridge-like beverage, consumed through straws to avoid the sediment at the bottom.

The Sumerians held beer in high esteem, often associating it with divine favor. It was consumed during religious ceremonies, daily meals, and social gatherings. Beer was often referred to as "the drink of life," and its production was considered a gift from the gods. The Sumerians even established a goddess of brewing, Ninkasi, emphasizing the beverage's sacred status.

In addition to its symbolic significance, beer also played a critical economic role in Mesopotamian society. Workers, especially those laboring on monumental construction projects, were often compensated with rations of beer, which served as both nourishment and a form of payment. This practice not only facilitated labor but also stimulated the economy, as the production and distribution of beer became central to trade and commerce.

Similarly, in ancient Egypt, beer was a foundational aspect of daily life and culture. Archaeological evidence suggests that beer brewing in Egypt dates back to around 4,000 BCE. The Egyptians brewed a variety of beers, with distinctive flavors and textures, often using emmer wheat, barley, and various herbs. Beer was consumed by all social classes, from laborers to pharaohs, and was a common offering to the gods during religious rituals.

Beer in ancient Egypt was intrinsically linked to health and fertility. It was often given to women during childbirth to promote strength and vitality. The Egyptians also recognized the nutritional value of beer, which provided essential calories and hydration. It was a common beverage for children and adults alike, consumed daily and featured prominently in their diet.

The significance of beer transcended mere consumption; it was also a vital aspect of social life. Just as in Mesopotamia, beer was a common feature at feasts and celebrations, often accompanying bread and other staple foods. The Egyptians held large communal feasts where beer flowed freely, reinforcing social bonds among participants and fostering a sense of community.

Both Mesopotamia and Egypt illustrate how beer was not simply a beverage but a complex cultural artifact that shaped social structures, economic systems, and religious practices. The legacy of these ancient civilizations can be seen in the continued global significance of beer today, where its production and consumption remain intertwined with societal values and traditions. The earliest evidence of beer in these regions serves as a testament to humanity's longstanding relationship with this ancient brew, which has evolved but never lost its place in the tapestry of human culture.

The Social Role of Beer in Early Civilizations

Beer, one of humanity's oldest beverages, played a pivotal role in the social fabric of early civilizations. Its significance transcended mere sustenance; it was deeply woven into the cultural, spiritual, and economic threads of societies across the globe. In examining the social role of beer in ancient cultures, we uncover its multifaceted functions that influenced social interactions, community bonding, and ritualistic practices.

A Beverage of Community and Hospitality

In early civilizations, beer served as a cornerstone for communal gatherings and hospitality. The act of brewing and sharing beer was often a communal effort, fostering bonds among individuals within a community. In Ancient Mesopotamia, for instance, beer was not only a dietary staple but also a medium for social interaction. Sumerians would gather in taverns, known as "bitu," where beer was consumed and stories shared. These establishments acted as social hubs, reinforcing community ties and providing a space for dialogue and merriment.

The importance of beer as a social lubricant can also be seen in ancient Egypt, where it was a common practice to offer beer to guests as a sign of hospitality. The Egyptians brewed various types of beer, often flavored with herbs and spices, to accommodate different tastes and occasions. Sharing beer at feasts and festivals was a way to strengthen relationships and solidify social hierarchies, as the wealthier members of society would often provide more lavish brews for their guests.

Beer and Rituals

Beer's role extended beyond daily life into the spiritual and ritualistic realms. In many ancient cultures, beer was considered a gift from the gods. The Sumerians, for example, had a goddess of beer, Ninkasi, who represented the brewing process and was revered in hymns and rituals. Beer was often offered in religious ceremonies, emphasizing its sacred status and reinforcing the connection between the divine and the community.

In ancient Egypt, beer was integral to funerary rites and offerings to the deceased. It was believed that providing beer for the afterlife would ensure the comfort and sustenance of the departed, showcasing the beverage's significance in both life and death. The ritualistic use of beer helped to define social roles within these cultures, as certain groups, like priests and leaders, would oversee the brewing and distribution of beer in ceremonial contexts, further solidifying their status within the hierarchy.

Economic and Social Exchange

Beer also played a vital role in economic exchange and trade. In Mesopotamia, beer was often used as a form of currency, with standardized amounts exchanged for goods and services. The brewing process was labor-intensive, and communities relied on skilled brewers, often women, to produce beer for trade and consumption. This not only provided economic opportunities for individuals but also reinforced social structures, as brewing became a respected craft.

Furthermore, the production of beer encouraged agricultural development, particularly the cultivation of barley and other grains. This agricultural expansion contributed to the growth of settlements and the formation of complex societies, as surplus production allowed for specialization of labor and the rise of trade networks. Beer became a commodity that facilitated relationships between neighboring communities, establishing bonds through trade and social interactions.

Conclusion

In summary, the social role of beer in early civilizations was profound and multifaceted. It served as a catalyst for community bonding, a medium for hospitality, a sacred offering in rituals, and an economic commodity that fostered trade and agricultural development. The cultural significance of beer transcended its function as a beverage, marking it as an essential element in the tapestry of human civilization. As societies evolved, the customs surrounding beer continued to adapt, but its fundamental role in fostering social connections remains a timeless aspect of human interaction.

The Ingredients: Barley, Water, and Yeast

Beer, often referred to as "liquid bread," is a diverse beverage that has captivated cultures throughout history. At its core, the brewing process involves three primary ingredients: barley, water, and yeast. Each of these components plays a crucial role in the flavor, aroma, and character of the final product.

Barley: The Backbone of Beer

Barley is the most common grain used in beer production. Its suitability for brewing lies in its unique composition, particularly its starch content and enzymatic properties. When barley grains are malted, they undergo a process of germination and drying that activates enzymes capable of breaking down starches into fermentable sugars. This sugar conversion is essential, as it provides the necessary fermentables that yeast will later convert into alcohol and carbon dioxide during fermentation.

There are various types of barley used in brewing, with two-row and six-row barley being the most prevalent. Two-row barley typically has a higher starch content, making it ideal for producing lighter beers, while six-row barley has a higher protein content and is often used in the production of ales and stouts. The malting process also imparts different flavors and colors to the beer, depending on the degree of roasting. For instance, pale malts yield light-colored beers, while darker roasted malts contribute rich, roasted flavors to stouts and porters.

Water: The Unsung Hero

Water is often overlooked in discussions about beer ingredients, but it is the most abundant component of beer, making up approximately 90-95% of the final product. The mineral content of water can significantly influence the taste and style of the beer. Different regions have varying water profiles, leading to distinct beer characteristics based on the water's mineral composition, including hardness, alkalinity, and the presence of specific ions such as calcium, magnesium, and sulfate.

Brewers often adjust their water chemistry to suit the type of beer they are producing. For example, a higher sulfate content can enhance hop bitterness in pale ales, while a balanced mineral profile is often preferred for lagers. The pH of the water also plays a role in the efficiency of the mash process, impacting sugar extraction and overall fermentation.

Yeast: The Fermentation Catalyst
Yeast is the living organism responsible for fermentation, converting sugars into alcohol and carbon dioxide, which gives beer its characteristic effervescence. The most common yeast used in brewing is Saccharomyces cerevisiae, known as ale yeast, which ferments at warmer temperatures, producing fruity and complex flavors. Lager yeast, on the other hand, Saccharomyces pastorianus, ferments at cooler temperatures and typically yields cleaner, crisper beers.

Brewers select specific yeast strains based on the desired flavor profile and characteristics of the beer. Different strains can produce varying levels of esters and phenols, which contribute to the aroma and flavor complexity. For instance, some yeast strains may impart banana or clove notes in wheat beers, while others might produce subtle apple or pear flavors in certain ales.

The Interplay of Ingredients
The interaction between barley, water, and yeast creates a harmonious blend that defines the essence of beer. The malt provides the sugars, the water shapes the brewing process, and the yeast transforms those sugars into alcohol and carbon dioxide, ultimately crafting a beverage that is both rich in history and varied in flavor.

Understanding the significance of these three ingredients allows beer enthusiasts to appreciate the artistry behind brewing. From the choice of barley to the manipulation of water chemistry and the selection of yeast strains, each decision influences the final product, showcasing the brewer's skill and creativity. This intricate relationship among barley, water, and yeast not only highlights the science of brewing but also celebrates the cultural heritage embedded in the age-old practice of beer making.

How Beer Spread Across Continents

Beer, one of humanity's oldest beverages, has a rich history that transcends geographical boundaries and cultural contexts. Its spread across continents is a testament to both human ingenuity and the universal appeal of this fermented drink. The journey of beer from ancient Mesopotamia to the modern world reflects not only advancements in brewing techniques but also the interconnectedness of societies through trade, colonization, and cultural exchanges.

Ancient Origins and Trade Routes

The earliest evidence of beer production dates back to around 5,000 BCE in Mesopotamia, where the Sumerians brewed a variety of ales using barley. As trade routes developed, notably the Silk Road connecting the East and West, beer began to travel beyond its point of origin. Merchants and travelers carried grains and brewing knowledge, introducing beer to new regions. This exchange was significant in places like ancient Egypt, where beer became integral to social and religious life, often consumed by workers who built the pyramids.

The Influence of Ancient Civilizations

Across continents, beer adapted to local tastes and available ingredients. In East Asia, especially in China, rice-based fermentation processes led to the production of early forms of beer-like beverages, such as huangjiu. Meanwhile, in Africa, indigenous brewing practices emerged, utilizing sorghum, millet, and maize. This regional diversity showcased beer's flexibility and its ability to integrate with local cultures.

As the Roman Empire expanded, so too did the popularity of beer. Romans, initially more inclined toward wine, encountered beer through their interactions with Germanic tribes. The Roman military and trade routes facilitated the spread of beer across Europe, leading to its acceptance and integration into various European cultures.

The Middle Ages and Brewing Guilds

By the Middle Ages, brewing had become a staple of daily life in Europe. Monasteries played a crucial role in the preservation and advancement of brewing knowledge, producing beer not only for their communities but also for trade. The establishment of brewing guilds during this period standardized production practices and quality, ensuring that beer became a respected commodity. This era saw the emergence of hops as a key ingredient, enhancing flavor and preservation.

The Age of Exploration and Colonialism

The Age of Exploration in the 15th and 16th centuries marked a significant turning point for beer. European colonizers brought their brewing traditions to the New World and beyond. In colonial

America, settlers adapted their brewing practices to local ingredients, resulting in a distinctive American beer culture. The popularity of beer surged, particularly during the American Revolution, as it became a symbol of independence and resistance against British rule.

Industrialization and Globalization

The Industrial Revolution in the 18th and 19th centuries transformed beer production with technological advancements in brewing equipment and transportation. The emergence of lager beer, which was easier to mass-produce and distribute, coincided with the growth of cities and immigration. German immigrants played a pivotal role in introducing lager to the United States, establishing breweries that catered to a burgeoning beer market.

As globalization progressed in the 20th century, multinational corporations emerged, consolidating beer production and distribution. The rise of global brands made beer accessible in nearly every corner of the world, while local craft brewing movements began to flourish, emphasizing regional flavors and traditional brewing methods.

Conclusion

Today, beer is a global phenomenon, enjoyed in diverse forms and styles across continents. Its journey from ancient Sumerian taverns to modern craft breweries illustrates not only the beverage's adaptability but also its ability to bring people together, fostering community and cultural exchange. The global spread of beer is a remarkable narrative of human creativity and connection, reminding us that this simple drink has played a significant role in shaping societies throughout history.

Chapter 2

Beer in Ancient Civilizations

Beer in Mesopotamian Culture

Beer is deeply woven into the fabric of Mesopotamian culture, particularly among the Sumerians and Babylonians, two of the earliest civilizations to inhabit the region that corresponds to modern-day Iraq. This ancient beverage played a multifaceted role, serving not only as a staple in daily life but also as a significant element in social, religious, and economic practices.

The Origins of Brewing in Sumer

The Sumerians, who thrived around 4500 to 1900 BCE, are often credited with some of the first known records of beer production. Archaeological evidence suggests that they brewed beer as early as 3500 BCE. The Sumerians made a variety of beer; they produced different styles by modifying the fermentation process and the ingredients used. Barley was the primary grain, which, when malted and mixed with water, created a thick, porridge-like substance. This was fermented using wild yeast, resulting in a nutritious and intoxicating beverage.

The Sumerians' reverence for beer is perhaps best exemplified in the "Hymn to Ninkasi," a Sumerian poem dating back to around 1800 BCE. This ancient text serves as both a prayer to Ninkasi, the goddess of beer, and a detailed recipe for brewing beer, highlighting its cultural significance. The hymn illustrates not only the practical aspects of brewing but also the spiritual connection the Sumerians had with beer, viewing it as a divine gift that facilitated social interactions and communal gatherings.

Social and Economic Significance

Beer was not merely a beverage; it occupied a central role in Sumerian society. It was consumed by all classes—men, women, and even children—and was often enjoyed during meals, celebrations, and religious rituals. The Sumerians developed a complex brewing industry, with women frequently taking on the role of brewers. Beer was also used as a form of currency; it was often offered as payment to laborers, particularly those working on large state projects, such as the construction of temples and ziggurats.

In addition to its role in daily life, beer was crucial in fostering social bonds. Sharing a drink was a common practice, symbolizing friendship and hospitality. The presence of beer in social gatherings would have facilitated conversation and community cohesion, making it an essential part of Sumerian culture.

The Babylonian Influence
As the Sumerians transitioned into the Babylonian era (circa 1894-539 BCE), the brewing tradition continued to flourish. The Babylonians inherited and expanded upon Sumerian brewing techniques, producing a wider variety of beer and refining brewing methods. They developed more sophisticated brewing equipment and began to document their processes more rigorously, leading to improved quality and consistency.

Babylonian society also reflected the importance of beer through its legal codes. The famous Code of Hammurabi, established around 1754 BCE, included regulations concerning the sale of beer, ensuring fair pricing and quality control. This legal recognition of beer underscores its economic value and the necessity of maintaining standards in its production and sale.

Rituals and Religion
In both Sumerian and Babylonian cultures, beer had a profound religious significance. It was frequently used in offerings to deities, particularly during rituals and festivals. Priests would often partake in beer to celebrate religious ceremonies, further intertwining the drink with the divine. The consumption of beer was not just a mundane activity; it was believed to connect individuals with the gods, fostering a sense of spirituality in everyday life.

In summary, beer in Mesopotamian culture, particularly among the Sumerians and Babylonians, was far more than a mere beverage. It was a vital element that influenced social structures, economic practices, and religious beliefs. The legacy of their brewing traditions continues to resonate today, marking the significance of beer in human civilization's historical journey.

The Role of Beer in Ancient Egyptian Society
In ancient Egyptian society, beer was more than a mere beverage; it was a fundamental element of daily life, culture, and economy. Archaeological findings and historical texts indicate that beer production and consumption were deeply embedded in the fabric of Egyptian civilization from the earliest dynasties, and its significance spanned social, religious, and economic realms.

Daily Nutrition and Consumption
Beer was a staple in the Egyptian diet, serving as a primary source of nourishment for the masses. Made primarily from barley and emmer wheat, the beer of ancient Egypt was typically unfiltered, resulting in a cloudy appearance rich in nutrients. This beverage was not only refreshing but also calorically dense, providing essential vitamins and minerals that

complemented the diet, which was often low in protein. Commonly consumed by people of all social strata, beer was integral to the meals of workers, farmers, and families alike.

Beer was routinely consumed with bread, another staple of the Egyptian diet, and was often used to celebrate the conclusion of a day's labor. In fact, records indicate that laborers, particularly those who worked on monumental projects such as the pyramids, were provided daily rations of beer as part of their compensation. This practice underscored the recognition of beer's role in sustaining labor and productivity, making it a vital aspect of the socio-economic structure.

Social and Cultural Significance

Beyond its nutritional value, beer served as a social lubricant within Egyptian society. It was customary to drink beer during gatherings, feasts, and celebrations, fostering community ties and camaraderie. The communal aspect of beer consumption was highlighted in various social scenarios, from family meals to larger communal festivities. Beer was often shared from a common vessel, symbolizing unity and friendship.

Moreover, the Egyptians attributed a sacred quality to beer, associating it with several deities. The goddess Hathor, who represented fertility, motherhood, and joy, was often depicted with a sycamore tree, symbolizing sustenance, and was closely linked to beer. Ritualistic offerings of beer were common in religious ceremonies, where it was presented to the gods to ensure their favor and blessings. The act of brewing beer also had ritualistic significance, with many brewing processes infused with prayers and offerings.

Beer in Rituals and Economy

In addition to its everyday use, beer held a prominent role in various Egyptian rituals and ceremonies, including funerals and religious festivals. It was believed that offering beer to the deceased ensured their comfort in the afterlife. Beer was also a significant part of the annual harvest festival, where offerings were made to the gods in gratitude for their bounty.

Economically, beer production was a substantial industry in ancient Egypt. Large-scale breweries were established, often run by temples or estates, which produced beer for both local consumption and trade. The standardization of beer quality and measurements led to its use as a form of currency in some transactions. The importance of beer in trade is evidenced by its inclusion in economic texts, where it was recorded as a commodity exchanged for goods and services.

Conclusion

In summary, beer in ancient Egyptian society was not merely a drink; it was a multifaceted element that influenced daily life, social interactions, and religious practices. Its integral role in nutrition, community bonding, and spirituality illustrates the profound impact that beer had on the ancient Egyptians. As both a sustenance and a symbol of social and divine connection, beer epitomized the complexities of Egyptian culture and continues to be a fascinating subject of study in the history of human civilization.

Beer and Rituals: Religious and Ceremonial Use in Ancient Cultures

Throughout history, beer has occupied a significant place not only as a beverage but also as a cultural artifact deeply interwoven with the social and spiritual fabric of ancient civilizations. Its production and consumption often took on ritualistic dimensions, with various cultures employing beer in religious ceremonies, offerings, and communal events that underscored its role in their belief systems.

In ancient Mesopotamia, beer was not merely a source of sustenance but a vital element in religious practices. The Sumerians, who are credited with some of the earliest documented brewing techniques, viewed beer as a divine gift. The Hymn to Ninkasi, a Sumerian poem dating back to around 1800 BCE, serves as both a prayer and a recipe for brewing beer, indicating the beverage's sacred status. Ninkasi, the goddess of beer, was celebrated through rituals that often involved offerings of beer to the deities during festivals. These ceremonies not only honored the gods but also reinforced communal ties among participants, who would share in the consumption of beer as a symbol of social unity and divine favor.

In ancient Egypt, beer played a similarly important role in religious and ceremonial contexts. The Egyptians brewed a variety of beer, which was consumed by all social classes and included in daily diets as a staple. Beer was often offered to the gods and featured prominently in funerary practices. Archaeological findings have revealed that beer was included in burial tombs, intended to provide comfort and sustenance for the deceased in the afterlife. Additionally, the consumption of beer during religious festivals, such as the annual Wepet-Renpet festival, involved rituals of offering and sharing that reinforced the connection between the living and the divine.

Beer was also integrated into rites of passage and communal gatherings in various ancient cultures. In many indigenous societies, beer or fermented beverages served as a medium for celebrating life events, such as births, weddings, and harvest festivals. For example, in some tribes of North America, beer-like beverages were used in potlatch ceremonies, where the host would offer food and drink to guests as a demonstration of wealth and generosity. These gatherings often included spiritual elements, such as prayers or songs, elevating the act of drinking beer to a sacred experience.

Moreover, the use of beer in rituals extended beyond mere offerings; it was often employed in divination practices. In ancient societies, the fermentation process was sometimes viewed as a means of connecting with the spiritual realm. For instance, the act of brewing was sometimes believed to facilitate communication with ancestors or deities, with the resulting beer serving as a conduit for messages and blessings. This belief system highlights the intricate relationship between fermentation, spirituality, and communal identity.

In the context of ancient Chinese culture, beer-like beverages were utilized in sacrificial rituals. Archaeological evidence shows that fermented drinks made from grains were offered to ancestors and deities as a means of honoring them and seeking their favor. The importance of these beverages in ceremonial contexts underscores the universal theme of beer as a vehicle for social cohesion and spiritual expression across diverse cultures.

As we examine the role of beer in ancient rituals, it becomes evident that its significance transcended mere consumption; it was a powerful symbol of community, spirituality, and cultural identity. In various ancient civilizations, beer served as a medium for expressing gratitude, seeking divine favor, and reinforcing social bonds, highlighting its enduring legacy as a catalyst for connection and celebration in human societies.

The Discovery of Fermentation

The discovery of fermentation is a pivotal moment in the history of human civilization, representing a profound intersection of science, culture, and daily life. Fermentation, the metabolic process by which microorganisms like yeast convert sugars into alcohol, acids, and gases, has been a cornerstone of food and beverage production, particularly in the making of beer. This process not only transformed raw ingredients into consumable products but also laid the groundwork for advancements in food safety, nutrition, and culinary arts.

Scientific Understanding of Fermentation

The scientific understanding of fermentation began to take shape in the 19th century, notably through the work of French chemist Louis Pasteur. Pasteur's experiments in the 1850s and 1860s debunked the prevailing notion of spontaneous generation, demonstrating that microorganisms were responsible for fermentation and spoilage. He observed that yeast was crucial for the fermentation process, and his discovery of pasteurization—heating liquids to kill harmful bacteria—revolutionized the brewing industry and enhanced the shelf life of beer and other beverages.

Pasteur's work provided a framework for understanding the biochemical processes involved in fermentation. He identified that different yeast strains could yield different flavors and alcohol contents, paving the way for brewers to experiment with various ingredients and techniques. This scientific approach not only improved the quality of beer but also fostered a culture of innovation within the brewing community.

Cultural Impact of Fermentation
Culturally, the discovery of fermentation had far-reaching implications. In ancient societies, the brewing of beer was often intertwined with religious rituals and communal gatherings. The ability to produce beer allowed for the creation of social hubs—taverns and pubs—where people could gather, share stories, and celebrate life's milestones. Beer became a symbol of hospitality and community, reinforcing social bonds and facilitating cultural exchange.

Fermentation also played a critical role in the preservation of food. Before refrigeration, fermentation was one of the primary methods for extending the shelf life of perishables. It enabled ancient civilizations to store grains and fruits, transforming them into beer, bread, and other fermented products that could be consumed long after the harvest. This capability not only aided in sustenance during harsh winters but also encouraged agricultural practices and the cultivation of specific crops, such as barley and hops.

Fermentation in Tradition and Innovation
As societies evolved, so did their relationship with fermentation. By the Middle Ages, monasteries became centers of brewing excellence, where monks refined their techniques and recipes, ensuring the quality of beer served in their communities. These religious institutions preserved the knowledge of fermentation through turbulent times, passing down recipes and techniques that would influence future generations of brewers.

In the modern era, the craft beer movement has reignited interest in fermentation, with brewers experimenting with diverse yeast strains, adjuncts, and fermentation processes. This trend reflects a broader cultural shift toward artisanal, locally produced goods that emphasize quality, creativity, and sustainability. The resurgence of interest in fermentation has also extended beyond beer to encompass other fermented foods, such as kombucha, kimchi, and yogurt, highlighting the ongoing relevance and significance of this ancient practice.

Conclusion
In conclusion, the discovery of fermentation represents a fundamental milestone in both scientific inquiry and cultural evolution. It has transformed beer from a basic sustenance into a

complex beverage that embodies tradition, innovation, and community. As societies continue to evolve, the principles of fermentation will undoubtedly remain a vital aspect of culinary practices, enriching both our diets and our social experiences. The scientific understanding of fermentation, catalyzed by pioneers like Pasteur, has enhanced our appreciation for this ancient craft, ensuring that beer and other fermented products maintain their place at the heart of human culture.

Beer in Early European Societies: The Celts and Germanic Tribes

The early European societies, particularly the Celts and Germanic tribes, had a profound relationship with beer, which was not merely a beverage but a cornerstone of their social and cultural practices. Beer served as a vital component of communal life and was intertwined with their rituals, economy, and social structure.

The Celts and Their Brewing Traditions

The Celts, who inhabited regions across Western Europe including modern-day Ireland, Scotland, France, and parts of Spain, had a rich tradition of brewing that dates back to at least 500 BCE. They utilized local grains, such as barley and wheat, along with various herbs and fruits for flavoring, creating a diverse range of brews. Archaeological findings suggest that early Celts brewed their beer using rudimentary techniques, often in open containers, allowing natural fermentation processes to take place.

Celtic culture revered beer, considering it a gift from the gods. It played a central role in their feasts, celebrations, and family gatherings, where it was customary to share beer among guests as a gesture of hospitality. The Celts believed that beer brought communities together, fostering bonds among kin, and was often consumed during rituals and ceremonies, including seasonal festivals that celebrated the harvest or honored deities.

The Role of Beer in Germanic Tribes

Similar to the Celts, the Germanic tribes, spread across regions that now encompass Germany, Scandinavia, and the Netherlands, also had deep-rooted customs related to beer production and consumption. The Germanic peoples brewed beer using barley and other grains, employing techniques that involved mashing, boiling, and fermenting. Beer was often flavored with various botanicals, and some tribes had unique brewing practices that included the use of honey or fruits, giving rise to distinctive regional styles.

For the Germanic tribes, beer was not only a staple beverage but also a vital element in their social structure. It was consumed during gatherings, where it served as a means of reinforcing alliances and camaraderie among warriors and clans. The communal consumption of beer was often accompanied by storytelling and music, emphasizing the beverage's role in cultural expression. Moreover, beer was associated with rituals surrounding fertility and the changing of seasons, indicating its importance in both daily life and spiritual contexts.

Economic and Social Significance

The brewing of beer among the Celts and Germanic tribes had significant economic implications. It was common for communities to brew beer on a communal basis, where surplus production could be traded or used in bartering systems. This helped foster local economies and facilitated trade between tribes, thereby enhancing social cohesion and interaction.

In addition, the status of beer in these societies was often reflected in their social hierarchies. Leaders and chieftains would host feasts where beer was central to the festivities, showcasing their wealth and generosity. Such gatherings not only solidified social bonds but also served as platforms for political discourse and decision-making.

Conclusion

In summary, beer in early European societies, particularly among the Celts and Germanic tribes, was much more than a simple fermented beverage. It was a vital cultural artifact that shaped social structures, economic practices, and spiritual beliefs. Through communal brewing and consumption, beer fostered connections among individuals and communities, reflecting the intricate relationship these societies had with their environment and each other. As these traditions evolved, they laid the groundwork for the brewing practices that would continue to flourish throughout European history, influencing modern beer culture across the continent.

Chapter 3

Beer in the Middle Ages

Monks and Brewing: The Role of Monasteries in Beer Production

Throughout history, beer has been a significant part of human culture, and monasteries played an instrumental role in its production, particularly during the Middle Ages. The brewing tradition within monastic communities is not merely a historical footnote; it is a cornerstone of beer's evolution and the reason behind many brewing techniques and styles that exist today.

Historical Context

During the early medieval period, as Europe entered the Dark Ages, monasteries became centers of learning and agriculture. Monks, typically well-educated and skilled in various crafts, took on the responsibility of preserving knowledge, including the art of brewing. The fall of the Roman Empire led to a decline in urban life and the rise of rural monastic communities, where self-sufficiency was paramount. Monasteries often produced their own food and drink, including wine and beer, to sustain their inhabitants and guests.

Brewing Practices

Monks used local ingredients to brew beer, primarily barley, hops, and water. They often experimented with different recipes and brewing methods. Monastic brewing was characterized by a commitment to quality and purity, as monks viewed brewing as a sacred act. The Trappist monks, in particular, became synonymous with high-quality beer production. They adhered to strict brewing guidelines, ensuring that each batch was made with care and precision.

In many cases, the brewing process involved an almost ritualistic element. Monasteries would often brew beer in large quantities to serve as both sustenance and a source of revenue. The surplus was sold to support the monastery's charitable activities and to fund the construction and maintenance of monastic buildings. This commercialization of beer laid the groundwork for the brewing industry as we know it today.

Economic and Social Impact

The economic model of beer production in monasteries contributed significantly to local economies. Monastic brews were often of such high quality that they made their way to local markets, fostering trade and commerce. Monasteries became important hubs of social interaction, as their taverns provided a place for locals to gather, share news, and strengthen community ties. The consumption of beer became intertwined with communal life, and the monasteries played a vital role in shaping and promoting beer culture.

Moreover, during times of fasting, monks would consume beer as a substitute for solid food, believing it to be a nutritious source of sustenance. This practice highlighted the importance of beer not only as a beverage but also as a vital nutritional resource.

Influence on Brewing Techniques
The brewing practices established by monks led to several innovations and standards that shaped the future of beer production. The introduction of hops as a preservative and flavoring agent is one of the most notable contributions. While earlier brewing relied on various herbs and spices, monks recognized the advantages of hops, which helped improve the shelf life and stability of the beer.

Monastic brewing also resulted in the development of distinct beer styles that are still celebrated today. For example, Trappist ales are renowned for their complexity and depth of flavor, often brewed with specific yeast strains cultivated by the monks. The techniques developed by these religious communities laid the foundation for modern brewing practices, emphasizing cleanliness, fermentation control, and flavor balance.

Conclusion
In summary, the role of monasteries in the history of beer production cannot be overstated. Monks not only preserved and refined brewing techniques but also contributed to the economic and social fabric of medieval Europe. Their commitment to quality and innovation established a legacy that continues to influence the brewing industry today, making them pivotal figures in the story of beer. As we enjoy a cold brew, we can appreciate the centuries of tradition and dedication that monks have contributed to this beloved beverage.

The Influence of Religion: Brewing in Christian and Islamic Cultures
The brewing of beer has woven itself intricately into the tapestry of human civilization, with its practices reflecting cultural, social, and religious dimensions. Among these, the influence of religion, particularly Christianity and Islam, has significantly shaped the brewing traditions and attitudes toward beer throughout history.

Brewing in Christian Cultures
In Christian cultures, beer has historically been viewed through a dual lens: as a blessing and a tool for community building. Monasteries emerged as key centers of brewing in medieval Europe, particularly during the Middle Ages. Monks, who adhered to a life of asceticism and

service, found brewing beer a practical means of sustenance. The Trappist monks, for example, established some of the most renowned breweries in Belgium, crafting high-quality beers that have become synonymous with the region's culture.

Beer served not only as nourishment but also as a social lubricant in Christian communities. It was often consumed during religious feasts and celebrations, where it played a role in fostering fellowship among congregants. Additionally, beer was an important aspect of the daily diet for many, particularly in regions where water quality was poor. The fermentation process involved in brewing beer effectively made it safer to drink, as the alcohol content could kill off harmful pathogens.

The influence of Christianity on brewing is also reflected in the establishment of brewing guilds and regulations that emerged during the medieval period. These guilds were often sanctioned by the Church and played a crucial role in ensuring quality and adherence to brewing standards, reinforcing the notion of beer as a divine gift meant to be respected and enjoyed.

Brewing in Islamic Cultures
In stark contrast, the brewing of alcohol, including beer, is explicitly forbidden in Islamic cultures due to religious tenets outlined in the Quran. The prohibition stems from the belief that intoxicants can lead to moral decay and social discord. The Quran states, "O you who have believed, indeed, intoxicants, gambling, [sacrificing on] stone alters [to other than Allah], and divining arrows are but defilement from the work of Satan, so avoid it" (Quran 5:90). As a result, the consumption of beer and other alcoholic beverages is considered haram (forbidden).

However, this does not mean that the tradition of brewing entirely vanished in Islamic regions. Instead, the brewing process was often redirected towards producing non-alcoholic beverages. For example, the use of grains like barley and millet continued, but the focus shifted to creating drinks like nabiz, a non-alcoholic fermented beverage made from dates or raisins, which was acceptable within Islamic dietary laws.

Moreover, the influence of Islam on beer and brewing can also be observed in the cultural attitudes toward social gatherings and hospitality. While alcohol is prohibited, the essence of community and sharing remains central. Coffee, tea, and other non-alcoholic beverages became cultural staples in Islamic societies, fulfilling similar social roles that beer once occupied in Christian contexts.

Conclusion

The interplay between religion and beer reveals a rich history of cultural adaptation and transformation. In Christian cultures, beer evolved into a communal beverage with deep social and spiritual significance, while in Islamic cultures, the prohibition of alcohol led to the innovation of alternative drinks that maintained the essence of hospitality and community. Understanding the religious influences on brewing not only highlights the diversity of beer traditions but also underscores the broader connections between culture, belief, and social practices throughout history.

The Development of Hops: A Key Ingredient in Beer

Hops are one of the four essential ingredients in beer, alongside water, malted barley, and yeast. Their development has been crucial to the evolution of brewing, significantly affecting the flavor, aroma, stability, and preservation of beer. Understanding the role of hops in beer production requires delving into their botanical characteristics, historical significance, and the technical advances that have allowed brewers to harness their full potential.

Botanical Origins and Characteristics

Hops, scientifically known as Humulus lupulus, are climbing plants from the Cannabaceae family. The female flowers of the hop plant, known as cones or strobiles, contain lupulin, a yellow resin that is rich in alpha and beta acids, essential oils, and other compounds that impart distinct flavors and aromas to beer. The bitterness provided by the alpha acids is crucial in balancing the sweetness of malt, while the essential oils contribute to the beer's aroma profile.

The cultivation of hops dates back to at least the 9th century in Europe, although some evidence suggests that they may have been used even earlier. Hops thrive in temperate climates, and regions with suitable growing conditions, such as Germany, the Czech Republic, and the Pacific Northwest of the United States, have become renowned for their hop production.

Historical Significance

Before the widespread use of hops, brewers often relied on a variety of herbs and spices, known as gruit, to flavor their beers. Ingredients like heather, yarrow, and wormwood were commonly used until the introduction of hops as a preservative and flavoring agent. The transition to hops began around the 12th century in Germany, where the systematic cultivation of hops was first recorded. By the 15th century, the use of hops in brewing had spread across Europe, and the beverage began to evolve into what we recognize today as beer.

One of the key advantages of hops over traditional gruit was their natural preservative qualities. Hops contain antimicrobial properties that inhibit the growth of certain unwanted bacteria. This meant that beers brewed with hops could be stored for longer periods without spoiling, allowing for greater distribution and trade.

Brewing Techniques and Innovations
The brewing process involving hops has seen significant advancements over the centuries. Initially, hops were added early in the brewing process during the boiling phase, which maximized the extraction of bitterness. As brewing science progressed, brewers began to experiment with different hop varieties and timing of hop additions to achieve desired flavor profiles.

The introduction of dry hopping—a technique where hops are added during fermentation—has revolutionized the craft of brewing. This method enhances the aroma of beer without adding extra bitterness, allowing for a more nuanced flavor experience. Furthermore, recent innovations in hop breeding have led to the creation of new hop varieties with unique flavor characteristics, such as tropical fruit, citrus, and herbal notes.

The Craft Beer Movement and Hops
The late 20th century saw a resurgence of interest in hops as part of the craft beer movement. Craft brewers have embraced hops not just as a bittering agent but as a defining feature of their beers. Styles such as India Pale Ales (IPAs), which emphasize hop flavor and aroma, have gained immense popularity. This cultural shift has fostered a renewed appreciation for local and artisanal hops, driving demand for diverse hop varieties and encouraging brewers to explore creative brewing techniques.

Conclusion
Hops have evolved from a simple bittering agent to a complex ingredient integral to the flavor and character of beer. Their development has influenced brewing practices, shaped beer styles, and played a crucial role in the economic viability of the brewing industry. As brewers continue to innovate and experiment with hops, their legacy as a key ingredient in beer is sure to endure, promising exciting flavors and aromas for generations to come.

Beer and Daily Life in Medieval Europe
During the medieval period, beer was not merely a beverage; it was an integral component of daily life in Europe. From the bustling towns to the quiet countryside, beer served as a staple drink, offering a reliable source of hydration and nutrition for people of all ages. The cultural, economic, and social significance of beer in medieval Europe cannot be overstated.

Nutritional Value and Safety of Beer

One of the primary reasons for the widespread consumption of beer was its nutritional value. In an era when access to clean drinking water was often limited and sanitation practices were rudimentary, beer was seen as a safer alternative to water. The fermentation process kills off harmful pathogens, making beer more palatable and safer for consumption. Moreover, the grains used in brewing, primarily barley, provided essential nutrients, including carbohydrates, vitamins, and minerals. As a result, beer was often consumed with meals, serving as a hearty supplement to the otherwise meager diets of many peasants.

Social and Cultural Significance

Beer played a crucial role in the social fabric of medieval life. Taverns and alehouses were central to community interaction, acting as hubs for socialization, political discourse, and entertainment. These establishments were often the focal point of village life where people gathered to share news, celebrate festivals, and engage in communal activities. The atmosphere of the tavern was typically lively, filled with music, laughter, and the clinking of mugs, fostering a sense of camaraderie among patrons.

The importance of beer in social gatherings is exemplified by the traditions surrounding feasts and celebrations. Beer was an essential part of weddings, harvest festivals, and religious ceremonies. It was often brewed specifically for such occasions, with families or communities coming together to create large batches that would last throughout the festivities. This communal brewing not only highlighted the significance of beer in marking important life events but also reinforced social bonds within communities.

Brewing Practices

Brewing was primarily a domestic activity in medieval Europe, with women often taking on the role of brewers. In many households, brewing beer was a routine task, and recipes were passed down through generations. The process typically involved steeping grains in hot water, boiling the mixture with hops (which began to gain popularity during the later medieval period), and fermenting it with natural yeasts. This home-brewed beer varied in strength and flavor, depending on the ingredients and methods used.

As towns expanded and the demand for beer increased, brewing began to transition from home kitchens to larger commercial establishments. This shift led to the emergence of professional brewers who produced beer for sale, giving rise to the first brewing guilds. These guilds regulated brewing practices, ensuring quality and safety, and became influential in the economy and governance of towns.

Beer in the Economy

Beer was not just a beverage; it was also an economic commodity. Its production and sale contributed significantly to local economies. Farmers grew barley and hops, while laborers worked in the brewing trade. Taxes on beer sales provided revenue for local authorities, further intertwining beer with the socio-economic structure of medieval society.

Additionally, the currency of beer extended beyond simple transactions. Beer was often used as a form of payment or barter, particularly in rural areas where cash was scarce. This practice underscored the beverage's integral role in the day-to-day economic interactions of medieval life.

Conclusion

In summary, beer was woven into the fabric of daily existence in medieval Europe. It served not only as a crucial source of hydration and nutrition but also as a social lubricant, economic commodity, and cultural cornerstone. The reverberations of beer's significance during this period can still be traced in contemporary brewing traditions and social customs, highlighting its enduring legacy in European history.

The Rise of Brewing Guilds and Regulations

The medieval period in Europe marked a significant evolution in the production and consumption of beer, characterized by the establishment of brewing guilds and the implementation of regulations governing the brewing industry. This transformation was influenced by a confluence of social, economic, and political factors that shaped the brewing landscape and laid the groundwork for the modern beer industry.

The Emergence of Brewing Guilds

Brewing guilds began to form in the late Middle Ages, primarily in urban areas where the demand for beer was high. These guilds were associations of brewers who banded together to protect their interests, establish standards, and regulate the brewing process. The formation of guilds was not limited to brewers; they often included other stakeholders in the brewing process, such as maltsters, hop merchants, and innkeepers. The guilds served multiple purposes: they provided a platform for mutual support among brewers, facilitated the sharing of knowledge and techniques, and offered a means to maintain quality control in the production of beer.

One of the earliest and most notable guilds was the "Brewers' Guild of London," founded in 1290. Members of brewing guilds were typically required to adhere to specific guidelines regarding the quality of ingredients, brewing methods, and sanitation practices. This emphasis on quality not only helped to protect the reputation of the guild but also ensured that consumers received a consistent product. Moreover, guilds played a pivotal role in the economic landscape of towns, as they regulated prices and controlled competition among brewers.

Regulations and Quality Control

As the popularity of beer grew, so did the necessity for regulations to ensure safety and quality. Local governments began to impose laws governing brewing practices, focusing on several critical areas: the ingredients used, the brewing process, and the sale of beer. Guilds often worked in conjunction with municipal authorities to enforce these regulations, which included stipulations on the purity of beer and the prohibition of harmful additives.

One significant regulation was the "Reinheitsgebot," or the German Beer Purity Law of 1516, which dictated that only barley, water, and hops could be used in the brewing of beer. This law was a direct response to public health concerns about the quality of beer, which could be compromised by the use of inferior or unsafe ingredients. The Reinheitsgebot not only established a standard for beer production but also set a precedent for brewing regulations that would influence beer production for centuries.

Social and Economic Implications

The rise of brewing guilds and regulations had profound social and economic implications. On one hand, these guilds created a sense of identity and camaraderie among brewers, fostering a community that emphasized craftsmanship and tradition. On the other hand, the regulations imposed by these guilds and local governments helped to protect consumers, ensuring that the beer they consumed met specific quality standards.

Furthermore, the existence of brewing guilds contributed to the formation of local economies centered around beer production. As the guilds grew in prominence, they often held significant political power, influencing local governance and trade policies. This interaction between brewing guilds and authorities laid the foundation for the brewing industry's evolution into a commercial enterprise.

Conclusion

The rise of brewing guilds and regulations during the medieval period was a pivotal moment in the history of beer. As these organizations sought to maintain quality and regulate the burgeoning industry, they helped shape the social, economic, and cultural landscape of beer consumption. The legacy of brewing guilds continues to resonate today, as modern craft brewers often look back to these historical practices for inspiration and guidance in their pursuit of quality and community in the brewing process.

Chapter 4

Beer in the Renaissance and Enlightenment

The Rise of Commercial Breweries: Beer as an Industry

The rise of commercial breweries marked a significant transformation in the brewing landscape, elevating beer from a traditional craft to a booming industry. This evolution began in earnest during the late Renaissance and into the Enlightenment, driven by a combination of technological advancements, shifts in societal behaviors, and economic motivations.

Historically, brewing was predominantly a domestic activity. Beer was produced in homes and small community establishments, often for personal consumption or local trade. However, as urbanization increased in the 16th and 17th centuries, populations flocked to cities, creating larger markets for beer. This demographic shift was critical; it led to a growing demand for consistent, high-quality beer that could not be met by home brewing alone.

One of the most pivotal developments in the commercial brewing industry was the establishment of commercial breweries. These entities began to emerge in large urban centers across Europe, where economies of scale could be realized. Entrepreneurs recognized the potential for profit in brewing, leading to the founding of some of the first dedicated breweries. Among these were significant establishments in Germany, England, and the Netherlands, which began producing beer on a much larger scale than ever before. Notably, the introduction of the steam engine during the Industrial Revolution further propelled this growth, allowing for greater efficiency in production processes.

The burgeoning commercial breweries capitalized on technological innovations that facilitated mass production. The introduction of refrigeration, for example, revolutionized the brewing process, enabling lager beers to be produced year-round rather than limited to the cooler months. Additionally, advancements in transportation—such as railroads—allowed breweries to distribute their products over greater distances, effectively expanding their market reach.

Scientific developments also contributed to the rise of commercial breweries. The work of pioneers like Louis Pasteur in the 19th century not only improved the understanding of fermentation but also introduced pasteurization, a method that enhanced beer's shelf life and safety. These scientific advancements reassured consumers about the quality of commercially produced beers, fostering a culture of trust and preference for these products over traditional home-brewed varieties.

With the emergence of commercial breweries, the beer market began to diversify significantly. Breweries started to produce a wider array of styles and flavors, catering to the evolving tastes of consumers. This diversity was further fueled by the establishment of brewing guilds, which regulated quality and promoted competition among brewers. As a result, beer became not only a staple of daily life but also a symbol of regional pride, with specific styles becoming associated with particular locales—such as pale ales from England, pilsners from the Czech Republic, or bocks from Germany.

The commercialization of beer also led to the establishment of branding and marketing strategies. Breweries recognized the importance of distinguishing their products in a crowded marketplace, leading to the creation of logos, advertising campaigns, and the development of unique packaging. As beer consumption became intertwined with social activities and gatherings, breweries began to position themselves as integral to community life.

By the late 19th and early 20th centuries, the beer industry had solidified itself as a major economic force, contributing significantly to local and national economies. This period also saw the rise of large multinational brewing corporations, which further transformed the landscape of beer production and consumption globally.

In conclusion, the rise of commercial breweries fundamentally reshaped the beer industry, transforming it from a local craft into a global enterprise. Through technological advancements, scientific discoveries, and strategic marketing, beer evolved into a staple of modern society, reflecting not only changing consumer preferences but also the cultural and social dynamics of the times.

Scientific Discoveries: Louis Pasteur and the Pasteurization of Beer

The story of beer is one that intertwines with the annals of scientific discovery, and few figures loom larger in this narrative than Louis Pasteur. Born in 1822 in Dole, France, Pasteur was a chemist and microbiologist whose work fundamentally transformed the understanding of fermentation and the brewing process. His pioneering research not only enhanced the quality of beer but also set the stage for modern microbiology.

Before Pasteur's contributions, brewing was largely an empirical craft, with brewers relying on traditional methods that had been passed down through generations. However, issues such as spoilage and variability in taste plagued brewers, leading to inconsistent product quality. The prevailing belief at the time attributed these problems to spontaneous generation, a theory suggesting that life could arise from non-living matter. Pasteur challenged this notion through meticulous experimentation and observation.

In the 1850s, Pasteur began his investigations into the fermentation process. He discovered that yeast, a microorganism crucial to fermentation, was responsible for converting sugars into alcohol and carbon dioxide. However, he also observed that unwanted bacteria could contaminate the brewing process, leading to sour and off-flavors in beer. Pasteur's research illuminated the role of microorganisms in fermentation, providing a scientific framework that explained how and why beer could spoil.

The breakthrough came when Pasteur proposed a method to eliminate these undesirable bacteria: pasteurization. In 1864, he developed a thermal process that involved heating liquid to a specific temperature for a set period, killing harmful microorganisms while preserving the quality of the beverage. This technique was first applied to wine, but its implications for beer were profound. By applying pasteurization to beer, brewers could significantly extend shelf life and ensure consistency in flavor, making it more reliable for consumption.

The practical application of Pasteur's findings revolutionized the brewing industry. As pasteurization became widely adopted in the late 19th century, breweries began to produce beer that was not only more stable but also free from spoilage. This innovation coincided with the rise of industrial brewing, where mass production techniques necessitated consistency and quality control. Pasteur's work laid the groundwork for these advancements, turning brewing into a more scientific and less artisanal endeavor.

Furthermore, Pasteur's discoveries had broader implications beyond beer. His work contributed to the development of germ theory, fundamentally changing the way diseases were understood and leading to advancements in public health. The principles of pasteurization found applications in various sectors, including dairy and food preservation, underscoring the interconnectedness of different industries.

Despite the scientific rigor that Pasteur introduced to brewing, it is crucial to recognize that his techniques did not eliminate the artistry involved in beer production. Master brewers continued to infuse their creativity into recipes, blending flavors and experimenting with ingredients while relying on pasteurization to ensure the quality of their products.

In conclusion, Louis Pasteur's contributions to the science of brewing cannot be overstated. His discovery of the role of yeast in fermentation and the development of pasteurization transformed the beer industry, enhancing product quality, safety, and longevity. By marrying science with brewing, Pasteur not only improved the beverage itself but also paved the way for future innovations in the field. The legacy of his work continues to reverberate through the brewing community, reminding us that the history of beer is as much a story of science as it is of culture and tradition.

The Cultural Role of Beer in European Society

Beer has served as more than just a refreshing beverage throughout European history; it has woven itself into the very fabric of society, influencing social norms, traditions, and even political structures. From the hearty ales of ancient tribes to the craft brews of modern microbreweries, beer has played a pivotal role in shaping European culture.

Historically, beer was a staple in the daily diet of many Europeans, particularly in regions where safe drinking water was scarce. In medieval societies, it was not uncommon for people to consume beer with every meal, as it was often safer than water. This practice laid the groundwork for beer to become a communal beverage, fostering social interactions among family members and neighbors. Taverns and public houses emerged as crucial social hubs where individuals came together to share stories, celebrate milestones, and engage in political discussions. The significance of these gathering places cannot be overstated, as they acted as informal forums for public discourse, allowing for the exchange of ideas and a sense of community.

The influence of beer on social customs is evident in numerous cultural traditions across Europe. For instance, in Germany, beer festivals like Oktoberfest not only showcase regional brews but also celebrate Bavarian culture, drawing millions of visitors each year. These festivals foster a sense of identity and pride, uniting people through shared experiences centered around beer. Similarly, in Belgium, the tradition of brewing is deeply ingrained in the national identity, with various regions boasting unique styles and brewing methods that reflect local heritage.

Beer has also been integral to rites of passage and celebrations throughout European history. In many cultures, beer is a traditional offering in wedding ceremonies, symbolizing abundance and joy. It plays a role in marking special occasions, from religious holidays to national festivities, illustrating its versatility as a celebratory beverage. The act of toasting with beer is embedded in European culture, signifying goodwill, camaraderie, and shared happiness.

Moreover, beer has served as a canvas for artistic expression in European society. The intricate designs of beer labels, the branding of breweries, and even the architecture of pubs and breweries reflect the cultural nuances of their regions. Beer has inspired countless works of literature, music, and art, becoming a symbol of leisure and enjoyment. From the taverns that inspired Charles Dickens to the songs sung in pubs across the UK, beer has left an indelible mark on the creative landscape of Europe.

The relationship between beer and politics is another noteworthy aspect of its cultural significance. Historically, beer has been used as a political tool, with leaders leveraging its popularity to gain favor among the populace. Public houses have served as venues for political rallies and discussions, illustrating how beer can influence public sentiment and mobilize communities. Additionally, beer taxes have often stirred public outcry, showcasing how deeply intertwined beer is with the socio-political fabric of European society.

In modern times, the craft beer movement has reinvigorated the cultural landscape, encouraging a return to traditional brewing practices while fostering innovation. Microbreweries have emerged as vital players in local economies, contributing to a resurgence of regional pride and identity. Beer festivals celebrating craft brews are now commonplace, uniting communities and promoting a sense of belonging.

In summary, the cultural role of beer in European society is multifaceted, encompassing social, economic, artistic, and political dimensions. As a beverage that transcends time and borders, beer continues to evolve while remaining a cherished element of European heritage, reflecting the diverse identities and traditions of the continent. Its ability to bring people together, foster creativity, and even influence politics underscores beer's enduring significance in shaping European culture.

Beer and Trade: The Influence of Global Commerce

The evolution of beer as a significant global commodity is a fascinating narrative that intertwines with the fabric of trade, commerce, and cultural exchange. Beer has traveled through centuries, crossing borders and oceans, morphing from a local staple to an international market powerhouse. This transformation has been influenced by various factors, including trade routes, colonialism, industrialization, and globalization.

Historically, beer's role in trade can be traced back to ancient civilizations. Mesopotamians and Egyptians were among the first to brew beer, and it quickly became a staple in their societies, functioning not only as a nutritional source but also as a medium of exchange. In these early economies, beer was often used as a form of payment for laborers, particularly those who worked on large-scale agricultural projects or construction, such as the pyramids. This practice highlights the intrinsic value beer held in these societies and its ability to foster economic activity.

As trade networks expanded, particularly during the Middle Ages, beer began to spread beyond its regional confines. The rise of monasteries in Europe played a pivotal role in this expansion. Monks meticulously refined brewing techniques, producing beer of higher quality that could be traded. Monastic brews became renowned, contributing to the local economies and establishing a burgeoning market for beer. Trade fairs and markets became focal points for the exchange of not only grains and ingredients but also finished beer products.

The Age of Exploration further propelled beer into a global commodity. As European powers established colonies in the Americas, Africa, and Asia, they brought their brewing traditions with them. The establishment of breweries in colonial territories not only catered to the tastes of European settlers but also adapted to local ingredients and brewing practices, leading to the creation of unique beer styles. This cross-pollination of brewing techniques and ingredients created a rich tapestry of beer culture that would influence local economies and trade patterns.

The Industrial Revolution marked a significant turning point in the commerce of beer. Advances in technology, such as refrigeration and pasteurization, allowed for larger-scale production and longer shelf life, leading to mass distribution. The emergence of lager beer, which required specific fermentation conditions, changed the brewing landscape and became immensely popular, particularly in Europe and the United States. With the introduction of railroads, beer could be transported over vast distances with unprecedented efficiency, allowing breweries to reach new markets and consumers far beyond their localities.

In the late 20th century, the globalization of beer took on new dimensions, driven by multinational brewing corporations. These companies expanded their reach into emerging markets in Asia, Africa, and South America, often adapting their marketing strategies to local tastes and preferences. This global commerce not only increased the availability of international beer brands but also created a competitive market that encouraged innovation and diversity in brewing practices.

Moreover, beer tourism has emerged as a significant facet of the beer trade, with festivals, brewery tours, and tasting events attracting enthusiasts from around the globe. This cultural exchange serves to promote local brews while fostering international appreciation for diverse beer styles, thereby enhancing the global beer market.

Today, beer stands as a symbol of cultural exchange and economic connection. The influence of global commerce on beer has not only shaped the industry but has also forged bonds between cultures. As consumers continue to seek unique and authentic beer experiences, the interplay between local traditions and global trade will likely continue to evolve, maintaining beer's status as a beloved beverage around the world.

Brewing Technology Innovations: From Barrels to Bottles

The journey of beer from its ancient origins to the modern era is marked not only by cultural evolution but also by significant technological advancements. Among the most remarkable innovations in the brewing industry is the transition from traditional storage methods, such as barrels, to contemporary bottling techniques. This transformation has had profound implications for the brewing process, distribution, and consumption of beer.

The Role of Barrels in Early Brewing

In the early days of brewing, particularly in ancient civilizations such as Mesopotamia and Egypt, beer was typically stored in clay vessels or wooden barrels. These barrels were crucial not just for storage but also for the fermentation process. The porous nature of wood allowed for some degree of oxygen exchange, which was beneficial for the fermentation of beer. However, it also posed certain challenges; the wood could impart flavors to the beer, and the barrels required careful maintenance to prevent spoilage and contamination.

As brewing practices evolved, so did the materials used for storage. The introduction of metal barrels, particularly during the Middle Ages, allowed for better regulation of temperature and improved hygiene. Metal barrels also facilitated the transportation of beer over longer distances, making it more accessible to a broader audience.

The Advent of Bottling

The shift to bottling beer began in earnest in the 17th century. The development of glassblowing techniques allowed for the production of sturdy glass bottles that could withstand the pressure of carbonated beer. This innovation was pivotal; bottles not only preserved the freshness and flavor of the beer but also provided a more convenient and portable option for consumers.

Bottles also allowed for a new marketing strategy. Breweries began to brand their products with labels, creating a visual identity that appealed to consumers. The ability to showcase the beer's color, clarity, and carbonation through the transparent glass became a powerful marketing tool.

Innovations in Bottle Design

As the demand for bottled beer grew, so did innovations in bottle design. The introduction of the crown cap in the late 19th century revolutionized bottling. Prior to this, corks were commonly used, which could lead to spoilage and inconsistent carbonation. The crown cap provided an airtight seal, significantly extending the shelf life of beer and ensuring that it retained its intended flavor profile.

Additionally, the development of different bottle shapes and sizes allowed breweries to target various market segments. For instance, the emergence of the "stubby" bottle in the 20th century appealed to a casual drinking culture, while larger, more ornate bottles became popular for craft and specialty beers.

The Impact of Pasteurization and Technology

Louis Pasteur's scientific discoveries in the 19th century also played a critical role in brewing technology. His work on fermentation and spoilage led to the process of pasteurization, which involves heating beer to kill harmful bacteria without significantly altering its flavor. This advancement not only improved the safety and stability of bottled beer but also facilitated its global distribution.

Furthermore, innovations in bottling technology, such as automated bottling lines, increased efficiency in production. These advancements allowed breweries to scale up their operations, leading to a boom in both craft and mass-produced beers.

Conclusion

The evolution from barrels to bottles in the brewing industry exemplifies how technology can transform not just a product but also the culture surrounding it. Bottling has enabled breweries to reach new markets, enhance the consumer experience, and ensure the quality of their products. As the brewing landscape continues to evolve, these innovations will undoubtedly play a crucial role in shaping the future of beer, allowing for greater experimentation and accessibility for beer enthusiasts worldwide. The story of beer is not just about ingredients and fermentation; it is also about the technologies that have allowed this ancient beverage to thrive in the modern world.

Chapter 5

Beer and the Industrial Revolution

The Impact of the Industrial Revolution on Brewing Processes

The Industrial Revolution, spanning from the late 18th century to the mid-19th century, was a transformative period that fundamentally changed many aspects of society, including the production and consumption of beer. As industrialization took hold, it introduced a wave of technological advancements, shifts in labor dynamics, and changes in consumer behavior that significantly impacted brewing processes.

Mechanization of Brewing

Before the Industrial Revolution, brewing was largely a manual and artisanal process, often conducted on a small scale within households or local breweries. The introduction of machinery revolutionized many aspects of beer production, leading to increased efficiency and consistency. Steam power became a critical component, allowing for the mechanization of tasks such as milling grains, boiling wort, and cooling beer. Equipment like steam-powered mash tuns and fermentation vessels enabled brewers to produce larger quantities of beer more rapidly than ever before.

This mechanization also paved the way for advancements in refrigeration and temperature control, which were crucial for brewing lagers. Prior to this, the fermentation process was highly dependent on ambient temperatures, resulting in considerable variability in beer quality. The ability to maintain consistent temperatures during fermentation led to the production of cleaner, crisper beers and marked a significant evolution in brewing practices.

The Role of Science in Brewing

The Industrial Revolution also saw the rise of a more scientific approach to brewing. The work of scientists such as Louis Pasteur in the mid-19th century was pivotal in understanding fermentation and the role of yeast. Pasteur's discoveries regarding microbial fermentation and spoilage allowed brewers to not only improve the quality of their beer but also to develop techniques for pasteurization, which extended the shelf life of beer and reduced spoilage during distribution.

As brewers began to appreciate the importance of yeast and fermentation, they experimented with different strains, leading to a broader range of flavors and styles. This scientific inquiry into the brewing process facilitated the rise of new beer types, particularly lagers, which became increasingly popular during this era.

Growth of Breweries and the Beer Industry
The Industrial Revolution also contributed to the growth of commercial breweries, transforming beer from a local, artisanal product into a mass-produced commodity. Larger breweries emerged, often employing hundreds of workers, and began to dominate the market. This shift facilitated economies of scale, allowing breweries to lower production costs and expand their reach. The establishment of railway systems enhanced the distribution of beer, making it possible for breweries to ship their products over longer distances, thereby broadening their market base.

Additionally, the rise of advertising and branding during the Industrial Revolution played a crucial role in shaping consumer preferences. Breweries began to develop distinct brand identities, utilizing marketing techniques to attract customers. This shift towards branding laid the groundwork for the competitive landscape of the beer industry that continues to evolve today.

Impact on Quality and Regulation
With the rise of large-scale production, concerns about quality and consistency became paramount. The Industrial Revolution prompted the introduction of regulations and standards for brewing practices, ensuring that consumers received a safe and reliable product. This regulatory environment helped to shape the modern beer industry, establishing benchmarks for quality that brewers are still expected to meet today.

In conclusion, the Industrial Revolution marked a significant turning point in the brewing industry, introducing mechanization, scientific advancements, and commercial practices that transformed how beer was produced and consumed. The innovations of this era not only increased the efficiency and scale of brewing but also laid the foundation for the diverse and rich beer culture we enjoy today. As breweries continue to evolve, they often reflect back on these historical changes, acknowledging their role in shaping the contemporary landscape of beer production and consumption.

The Emergence of Lager: A New Type of Beer
The emergence of lager in the 19th century marked a pivotal transformation in the brewing landscape, redefining beer production and consumption practices. Unlike ales, which had dominated brewing traditions for centuries, lagers introduced a new fermentation technique that capitalized on the unique properties of bottom-fermenting yeasts. This innovation

significantly influenced the flavor, aroma, and overall character of beer, ultimately leading to lager's widespread popularity worldwide.

The origins of lager can be traced back to Bavaria, Germany, where conditions favored the development of this distinct type of beer. The word "lager" itself comes from the German term "lagern," meaning "to store." Early lagers were brewed in the colder months and stored in cool caves or cellars, allowing for a slow fermentation process that occurred at lower temperatures, typically between 45°F and 55°F (7°C to 13°C). This lower fermentation temperature was made possible by the discovery of lager yeast (Saccharomyces pastorianus), a strain that ferments more slowly and settles at the bottom of the fermentation vessel, unlike its ale counterpart, which ferments at warmer temperatures and rises to the top.

The first documented lagers date back to the 15th century in Bavaria, but it wasn't until the 19th century that the style began to gain traction. One of the key figures in the rise of lager was Gabriel Sedlmayr, a brewer from the Spaten brewery in Munich, who is credited with refining the lager brewing process. Sedlmayr's innovations included advances in refrigeration technology and the introduction of pale malts, which contributed to the clean, crisp taste that characterized lagers. By the mid-1800s, the popularity of lager had spread beyond Germany, reaching Austria and eventually making its way to the United States, where German immigrants played a significant role in establishing brewing traditions.

Lager's ascent coincided with the Industrial Revolution, which brought about significant changes in brewing practices. The advent of industrial machinery and advancements in transportation facilitated the mass production and distribution of lager, making it accessible to a broader audience. Breweries began to adopt steam engines, which allowed for more efficient brewing processes and the ability to produce larger batches of beer. This period also saw the development of new packaging methods, such as the introduction of bottles and cans, which further expanded the market reach of lager.

By the late 19th century, lager had become the dominant beer style in many parts of the world, particularly in the United States. The light, refreshing profile of lagers appealed to a diverse audience, and breweries began to produce various styles, including Pilsners, Märzens, and Bocks, each with its distinct characteristics. The Pilsner, in particular, gained immense popularity after its creation in the Czech city of Pilsen in 1842, setting a new standard for lager brewing with its golden color and hoppy bitterness.

However, the rise of lager was not without challenges. The competition from ales, particularly in regions with strong brewing traditions, persisted. Additionally, during the Prohibition era in the

United States (1920-1933), many breweries that produced lagers were forced to close, while others pivoted to producing non-alcoholic beverages. Despite this setback, the post-Prohibition era saw a resurgence of lager, largely due to the efforts of German-American brewers who reintroduced traditional lager recipes and brewing techniques.

Today, lagers remain a cornerstone of global beer culture, appreciated for their versatility and range of flavors. From refreshing light lagers to robust dark lagers, this style has evolved and adapted, embodying the complexities of modern brewing while maintaining its historical roots. The emergence of lager not only transformed the beer industry but also laid the foundation for the global beer market, ensuring its place in the hearts and glasses of beer enthusiasts worldwide.

Mass Production and the Growth of Global Beer Brands

The industrial revolution marked a pivotal turning point in the history of beer, transforming it from a localized craft to a mass-produced commodity. This transition was facilitated by technological advancements, which allowed breweries to scale production while maintaining consistency and quality. The emergence of large-scale breweries in the late 19th and early 20th centuries set the stage for global beer brands that we recognize today.

One of the most significant innovations during this period was the development of refrigeration. Prior to refrigeration, brewing was heavily influenced by the seasons, limiting production and shelf life. The introduction of mechanical refrigeration allowed breweries to produce beer year-round, creating a stable supply and enabling brewers to experiment with different styles and flavors. This technology was especially crucial for lager production, which requires cooler fermentation temperatures. As a result, lagers became immensely popular, leading to their dominance in the beer market.

Another critical innovation was the advent of pasteurization, pioneered by Louis Pasteur in the mid-19th century. Pasteurization involved heating beer to kill off harmful microorganisms, which extended its shelf life and improved safety. This process not only allowed for longer distribution distances but also fostered the growth of brand recognition. Breweries could now ship their products across regions without the fear of spoilage, paving the way for national and eventually international brands.

The combination of these technological advancements, coupled with the rise of transportation systems like railroads, enabled breweries to distribute beer far beyond their local markets. The railways connected rural breweries with urban centers, facilitating the flow of beer to a growing population eager for affordable and accessible beverages. The proliferation of the beer-drinking culture coincided with industrialization, as more people moved into cities for work, leading to increased demand for refreshment options.

By the late 19th century, several breweries had grown to prominence, establishing themselves as household names. Anheuser-Busch, Miller, and Heineken are examples of companies that leveraged mass production techniques to expand their reach. These brands began marketing their beers not just as local products but as symbols of national identity, promoting their unique brewing traditions while capitalizing on the appeal of consistency and reliability.

Globalization further fueled the growth of these brands. As nations interacted through trade and cultural exchange, beer began to transcend borders. American breweries, influenced by German immigrants, adopted lager styles and production methods, leading to the establishment of a vibrant beer culture in the United States. Concurrently, European brands sought to enter the American market, resulting in a cross-pollination of brewing techniques and styles.

The mid-20th century saw the rise of beer advertising, which played a crucial role in shaping consumer perceptions. Large brewing companies invested heavily in marketing campaigns that emphasized brand loyalty and lifestyle associations, embedding beer within the fabric of social life. This era also witnessed the rise of beer as a symbol of leisure, with brands sponsoring sports events and music festivals, further entrenching their presence in popular culture.

However, the era of mass production also led to the homogenization of beer styles, as big brands prioritized consistency over diversity. This sparked a counter-movement in the late 20th century that emphasized craft brewing, leading to a renewed interest in unique flavors and locally produced beers. While mass production has laid the groundwork for the global beer market, the craft beer revolution has reshaped the landscape, encouraging consumers to explore a wider array of choices that reflect personal taste and regional characteristics.

In conclusion, mass production and the growth of global beer brands transformed the way beer is produced, marketed, and consumed around the world. While this shift brought about consistency and accessibility, it also paved the way for the craft beer movement, which continues to challenge the status quo and enrich the beer culture globally. Today, the beer industry stands at a crossroads, balancing the efficiency of mass production with the demand for quality and diversity that craft breweries champion.

The Role of Immigration in Beer's Spread: German Brewers in America

The history of beer in America is inextricably linked to the waves of immigration that shaped the cultural landscape of the nation. Among these immigrant groups, German brewers played a pivotal role in the establishment and proliferation of beer culture throughout the United States, particularly during the 19th century. Their contributions not only transformed the brewing industry but also influenced social customs, community dynamics, and the American palate.

The German Immigration Wave

The mid-19th century marked a significant influx of German immigrants to the United States, driven by factors such as political unrest, economic hardship, and the promise of a better life. Between 1820 and 1880, it is estimated that more than 5 million Germans settled in America, many of whom were skilled laborers, artisans, and brewers. This wave of immigration coincided with the rise of urban centers, particularly in the Midwest and Northeast, where these immigrants could establish their brewing businesses and find a ready market for their products.

Establishment of Breweries

German immigrants brought with them a rich brewing tradition characterized by the use of high-quality ingredients and specific brewing techniques. They introduced lager beer, a style that was relatively unknown in the U.S. at the time, preferring its crisp, clean taste over the ales that dominated the American beer market. The first commercial lager brewery in America, the Bavarian Brewery, was established in 1840 in Philadelphia, setting the stage for the lager revolution.

As German immigrants settled in cities like Milwaukee, St. Louis, and Cincinnati, they established numerous breweries that quickly became integral to their communities. By the 1850s, Milwaukee had emerged as the brewing capital of the U.S., home to notable breweries such as Pabst, Schlitz, and Miller. These establishments not only catered to the German populace but also began to attract a broader American audience, introducing lager as a popular beverage choice.

Cultural Impact and the Beer Garden

The influence of German brewers extended beyond just the production of beer; they played a crucial role in shaping social customs and community interactions. Beer gardens, a staple of German culture, became popular venues for social gatherings, fostering a sense of community and camaraderie among immigrants and locals alike. These spaces provided a welcoming atmosphere for people to enjoy food, music, and, of course, beer, often becoming hubs for cultural exchange.

Moreover, the beer gardens served as informal meeting places for discussions around politics and social issues, helping to integrate German immigrants into American society while preserving their cultural heritage. The establishment of these communal spaces facilitated the spread of beer culture, making it a social lubricant that transcended ethnic boundaries.

The Brewing Industry's Growth

The success of German breweries laid the groundwork for the broader American brewing industry. The techniques and practices introduced by German immigrants influenced brewing methods nationwide, leading to the rise of large-scale breweries that capitalized on the growing demand for beer. By the end of the 19th century, the United States had a thriving beer industry, with German-style lagers dominating the market.

However, the Prohibition era (1920-1933) presented significant challenges to the brewing industry, leading to the closure of many German-owned breweries. Despite this setback, the legacy of German brewers endured, as they had established a strong beer culture that would eventually resurface in the post-Prohibition landscape.

Conclusion

The role of German brewers in the spread of beer in America is a testament to the profound impact of immigration on cultural practices. Their contributions not only transformed the brewing industry but also enriched the social fabric of American life. Today, the influence of these early German immigrants can still be seen in the diverse beer offerings and brewing traditions that continue to thrive across the nation, as well as in the ongoing celebration of beer as a cherished component of American culture.

Beer in the Age of Railroads: Transportation and Distribution

The Industrial Revolution brought profound changes to the brewing industry, one of which was the advent of railroads. This transformative period in the 19th century not only revolutionized transportation but also had a lasting impact on the production, distribution, and consumption of beer. The intersection of railroads and brewing laid the groundwork for a burgeoning beer market, facilitating the growth of breweries and enabling the spread of beer culture across regions and nations.

Revolutionizing Distribution

Before the railroads, beer distribution was primarily local, limited by the constraints of horse-drawn carts and the availability of roads. Breweries often served their immediate communities, resulting in a lack of diversity in beer styles and choices. The introduction of railroads drastically altered this dynamic. Trains allowed for the rapid transportation of goods over long distances, enabling breweries to reach markets that had previously been inaccessible. This expansion not only increased sales for existing breweries but also encouraged the establishment of new breweries aiming to capitalize on the broader market.

Breweries began to utilize the rail system to ship their products quickly and efficiently, which was crucial for beer, a perishable product sensitive to temperature and time. Railroads facilitated the transport of kegs and bottles to urban centers, where demand for beer was surging due to population growth and industrialization. This expansion laid the foundation for a more competitive beer market, as breweries from different regions could now vie for customers far beyond their localities.

The Emergence of National Brands

As railroads connected cities and towns, breweries began to think beyond their local footprint. This shift led to the emergence of national beer brands. Major breweries, such as Anheuser-Busch and Pabst, recognized the potential of rail transport to distribute their products across states and into new markets. They invested in marketing strategies that promoted their brands nationally, utilizing railroads not just as a means of transport but as a lifeline for their growing enterprises.

With railroads enabling faster and more reliable transportation, breweries could also produce larger quantities of beer. The increased scale of production led to innovations in brewing processes and technology, allowing for consistent quality across batches. Standardization became vital as consumers began to expect the same taste and quality regardless of where they purchased their beer. As a result, beer brands became household names, and regional differences began to blur as consumers gravitated toward familiar labels.

Impact on Local Breweries

While larger breweries benefited from the railroad expansion, local breweries faced both challenges and opportunities. The influx of national brands created intense competition, pressuring smaller breweries to innovate and differentiate their products. Some local brewers began to emphasize unique regional ingredients and traditional brewing methods, cultivating a loyal customer base that appreciated local craftsmanship.

Moreover, railroads also contributed to the rise of beer tourism. Railroads not only transported beer but also beer enthusiasts eager to explore new breweries and beer styles. This fostered a culture of appreciation for craft beer, setting the stage for future movements in brewing that valued local and artisanal production.

Conclusion

The age of railroads marked a pivotal chapter in the history of beer, transforming how it was produced, transported, and consumed. With the ability to reach distant markets, breweries expanded their operations, leading to the creation of national brands and a more competitive beer landscape. As the railroads facilitated the distribution of beer, they also shaped the culture surrounding it, paving the way for the diverse and vibrant beer industry we see today. The legacy of this era is evident in the continued importance of transportation and distribution in the global beer market, as well as in the enduring popularity of local and craft breweries that arose in response to the changing dynamics of the beer industry.

Chapter 6

Beer in Colonial America

Beer in Early Settlements: Jamestown and Plymouth

The establishment of early American settlements such as Jamestown in 1607 and Plymouth in 1620 marked significant milestones in the history of colonial America. These settlements not only represented the aspirations of European settlers but also highlighted the integral role of beer in their daily lives and survival strategies. In an era when clean drinking water was often scarce and laden with pathogens, beer emerged as a vital staple, providing hydration and nourishment to the colonists.

Jamestown: The First Permanent English Settlement

Jamestown, the first permanent English settlement in North America, was established by the Virginia Company. The settlers arrived with a desire to cultivate tobacco for profit, yet they quickly faced numerous hardships, including conflicts with Indigenous peoples, a harsh environment, and food shortages. Among the provisions brought to the settlement, beer was included, as it was a common practice for Europeans to carry a supply of ale or beer on long voyages. This trend was partly due to the belief that beer was safer to drink than water.

Early records from Jamestown indicate that the settlers brewed their beer using local ingredients. They adapted their recipes to include corn, which was cultivated by Indigenous peoples, as well as other grains that were available. However, the brewing efforts were often hampered by the scarcity of resources and the need to prioritize survival over leisure. Despite these challenges, beer remained a crucial part of the settlers' diet, providing not only hydration but also calories and essential nutrients.

Plymouth: The Pilgrim Settlement

Similarly, the Pilgrims who settled at Plymouth faced a harsh reality upon arriving in the New World. The Mayflower carried a mix of supplies, including beer, which would become a mainstay for the settlers. Arriving in November, the Pilgrims faced a brutal winter, leading to high mortality rates and food shortages. The early community of Plymouth relied on the Indigenous peoples for assistance, and beer became a means of fostering relationships and trade.

The Pilgrims, like their Jamestown counterparts, understood the importance of beer in their diet. The presence of beer not only provided comfort during difficult times but also served as a social lubricant, facilitating gatherings and reinforcing community bonds. The Pilgrims brewed their beer using the grains they could procure, often experimenting with different local ingredients. The early American settlers recognized that brewing beer could be both a necessity and a communal activity, reinforcing social ties in an otherwise challenging environment.

Beer vs. Cider: Popular Drinks in Colonial Times
During this early period of settlement, beer coexisted with other alcoholic beverages, notably cider, which was also prevalent due to the abundance of apple orchards. In fact, both beer and cider were commonly consumed by people of all ages, as they were considered safer alternatives to water. The settlers often engaged in brewing both beverages, which became central to their social lives and culinary practices.

As these settlements began to thrive, the brewing traditions they established laid the groundwork for the burgeoning American beer culture. By the late 17th century, the first commercial breweries began to emerge in New England, reflecting the settlers' growing appreciation for beer as an integral component of their culture and economy.

In conclusion, beer played a vital role in the early American settlements of Jamestown and Plymouth. It served as a crucial source of hydration and nutrition, fostered community relationships, and laid the foundation for the development of a distinct American brewing tradition. The early colonists' reliance on beer exemplifies how this ancient beverage transcended mere consumption; it became a vital part of their survival, socialization, and ultimately, their cultural identity in the New World.

The Role of Beer in the American Revolution
The American Revolution, a pivotal moment in the history of the United States, was not only characterized by battles and political upheaval but also by the social and cultural elements that shaped colonial life. Among these, beer played a significant and multifaceted role in the lives of colonists, influencing social dynamics, fostering unity, and even impacting military strategy.

In the years leading up to the Revolution, beer was a staple beverage in colonial America. Unlike water, which was often unsafe to drink, beer was a more reliable source of hydration. It was consumed daily by people of all ages, serving as a dietary staple that offered nutritional benefits, especially when brewed with various grains. Beer was brewed at home and in taverns, creating a vibrant tavern culture that became central to social life. These establishments were not just places to drink but were also venues for political discourse and community gatherings, where individuals discussed grievances against British rule and shared ideas about independence.

As tensions escalated in the 1760s and 1770s with the imposition of taxes such as the Stamp Act and the Townshend Acts, beer emerged as a symbol of resistance. The heavy taxation of essential goods, including malt and imported spirits, incited anger among colonists who viewed these measures as an infringement on their rights. In response, many colonists boycotted British beer and spirits, opting instead to support local breweries. This not only fostered a sense of community but also promoted the burgeoning American brewing industry, which began to flourish as a result of the increased demand for locally produced beer.

One of the most notable events reflecting the role of beer in the Revolution was the Boston Tea Party of 1773. While the protest centered around tea, it was indicative of the larger anti-British sentiment that permeated colonial society. The slogan "no taxation without representation" resonated deeply within the taverns, where beer was consumed and discussions about freedom and rights were fervently debated. Taverns became hotbeds of revolutionary ideas, and many of the early leaders of the Revolution, including Samuel Adams and Paul Revere, were known to frequent these establishments.

Moreover, beer also played a tactical role during the Revolution. The Continental Army faced numerous challenges, including inadequate supplies and low morale. Beer was often used as a means to boost troop spirits, with officers providing soldiers with rations of beer to improve their morale and camaraderie. Additionally, the army's reliance on local breweries for supplies illustrated the importance of beer in sustaining the forces during prolonged campaigns. The brewing community stepped up to support the troops, often providing necessary resources to ensure their survival.

As the war progressed, the brewing industry became more organized. The establishment of local breweries not only provided sustenance for soldiers but also became a rallying point for nationalist sentiment. The brewing of beer became a patriotic act, and many brewers openly supported the revolutionary cause, creating beers that symbolized liberty and independence.

In conclusion, beer played a crucial role in the American Revolution, serving as a beverage of choice, a means of social cohesion, and a symbol of resistance against British rule. Its presence in taverns facilitated political discourse and unity among colonists, while its practical use in the military bolstered morale and camaraderie among soldiers. The transformation of beer from a simple staple to a symbol of rebellion illustrates the profound impact that this ancient beverage had on the fight for American independence.

Beer vs. Cider: Popular Drinks in Colonial Times

During the colonial era in America, beer and cider emerged as the two dominant alcoholic beverages, each reflecting the diverse cultural influences and agricultural practices of the time. Both beverages served not only as refreshment but also as crucial components of social life, economy, and health in early settlements.

Historical Context

In the early 17th century, the settlers of Jamestown and Plymouth arrived in a land abundant with natural resources, yet their drinking habits were heavily influenced by their European origins. Beer was a staple in England, where it had been consumed for centuries, while cider held a revered place in the diets of the English, particularly in the West Country. As the colonies developed, both beverages quickly became essential in the daily lives of the colonists.

Ingredients and Production

Beer production relied primarily on barley, water, hops, and yeast—ingredients that were increasingly available to settlers. Early colonial brewers often used local grains, such as corn and rye, adapting traditional European recipes to suit available resources. The brewing process was typically home-based and communal, with families and neighbors sharing the workload.

Cider, on the other hand, emerged from the abundance of apple orchards that thrived in various regions of colonial America. The first settlers brought apple seeds and saplings from Europe, and as apple cultivation expanded, so did the production of cider. The fermentation process was relatively simple, involving the juicing of apples followed by natural fermentation. This ease of production made cider an accessible drink for many households.

Popularity and Cultural Significance

While both beverages were widely consumed, their popularity fluctuated based on regional preferences and availability of ingredients. In New England, cider was particularly popular due to the region's favorable climate for apple growing. Cider houses became social hubs, where people gathered to drink, socialize, and conduct business. It was also a practical choice for many colonists; cider was often deemed safer than water, which could be contaminated.

Conversely, beer was notably prominent in urban areas and among groups that had a stronger European brewing tradition. Taverns that served beer became important social institutions, facilitating community interactions and the exchange of ideas. These establishments were often run by immigrants, who brought their brewing practices and preferences to the New World.

Economic Factors

The economic landscape of the colonies was also shaped by beer and cider production. The cultivation of barley for beer and apples for cider created agricultural opportunities, leading to the establishment of local markets and trade. Notably, beer became a significant economic driver in areas with established brewing traditions, while cider production thrived in regions rich in apple orchards.

Taxes and regulations surrounding the production and sale of beer and cider also played a role in their development. Governments recognized the importance of these beverages, implementing laws that affected brewing practices, such as licensing and taxation, which further influenced their popularity and economic impact.

Conclusion

In summary, beer and cider were more than just beverages in colonial America; they were integral to the social fabric, economy, and health of the early colonies. Cider's association with the agricultural bounty of the land and beer's ties to European traditions created a rich tapestry of drinking culture that varied by region. As the colonies grew, so too did the complexity and diversity of their alcoholic beverages, setting the stage for future developments in American brewing culture. The rivalry between beer and cider during this period laid the foundation for the modern beverage industry, reflecting the evolving tastes and practices of a burgeoning nation.

Brewing in the New World: The Challenges of New Ingredients

The establishment of breweries in the New World during the colonial era was a complex undertaking shaped by various factors, particularly the availability and suitability of local ingredients for brewing beer. While European settlers brought their brewing traditions and techniques with them, they quickly encountered challenges due to the differing agricultural landscapes and ecosystems of North America. This section delves into these challenges and their implications for early American brewing practices.

Adaptation to Local Grains

One of the primary challenges faced by colonists was the adaptation to the grains available in the New World. Barley, the staple grain for brewing in Europe, did not thrive in many colonial regions, particularly in the Eastern seaboard where the climate and soil conditions differed significantly from those in Europe. The settlers had to experiment with native grains such as corn, wheat, and rye. Corn, in particular, became an essential ingredient in early American brewing, leading to the creation of unique beer styles, such as corn beer, which differed significantly from the traditional European ales.

However, this adaptation was not without its challenges. Corn, while abundant, posed difficulties in the brewing process. Its high starch content required specific fermentation techniques to convert the starches into fermentable sugars. Early American brewers needed to innovate and modify traditional European brewing methods to accommodate these local ingredients, leading to a blend of old-world practices and new-world ingenuity.

Water Quality and Availability

Water quality and availability also presented significant challenges. In Europe, brewers often relied on specific water sources that contributed distinct flavors to their beers, influenced by local mineral compositions. In contrast, the New World featured a wide variety of water sources, each with different chemical profiles, which affected the taste and quality of the beer produced. Early American brewers often had to conduct experiments to determine the best water sources for their brewing needs, sometimes traveling long distances to access suitable water for brewing.

Moreover, the access to clean water was not always guaranteed, particularly in rapidly growing settlements where sanitation infrastructure was lacking. This situation led brewers to sometimes resort to less than ideal water sources, which could compromise the quality and safety of the beer. The importance of water chemistry in brewing was not fully understood at the time, and these experiments laid the groundwork for future advancements in brewing science.

Availability of Hops

Hops, a crucial ingredient for flavoring and preserving beer, were not as readily available in the New World as they were in Europe. The colonists initially imported hops from Europe, but this practice was costly and unsustainable. The search for local hop varieties became essential, leading to the discovery of native plants with similar flavoring properties, such as wild hops. However, these local varieties often lacked the stability and consistency that European brewers relied upon, posing challenges for brewers seeking to create a recognizable and consistent product.

As the brewing industry evolved in the New World, the cultivation of hops began to take root, particularly in areas with favorable climates like the Pacific Northwest. This shift not only improved the quality of beer produced but also aligned the New World brewing practices more closely with European traditions.

Conclusion

The challenges of new ingredients in the New World shaped the early American brewing landscape, leading to a unique fusion of techniques and flavors. By adapting to local grains, experimenting with water sources, and gradually cultivating hops, early American brewers paved the way for the rich and diverse brewing culture that would flourish in the centuries to follow. These adaptations not only ensured the survival of brewing practices in the New World but also contributed to the evolution of beer as a distinctly American tradition that continues to evolve today.

The First American Breweries: Foundations of a Brewing Nation

The history of beer in America is deeply intertwined with the nation's cultural and economic evolution, dating back to the early colonial period. As European settlers arrived in North America in the 17th century, they brought with them a rich brewing tradition. The first American breweries emerged in these settlements, laying the groundwork for a burgeoning industry that would flourish over the centuries.

The earliest documented brewery in America was established in 1632 in New Amsterdam (now New York City) by the Dutch West India Company. The brewery was created to satisfy the growing demand for beer among settlers and sailors. At the time, water was often contaminated, leading to health issues; beer, being fermented, was safer to drink. This necessity for a reliable source of beverage played a crucial role in the establishment of these early brewing operations.

By the mid-1600s, the Massachusetts Bay Colony also saw the emergence of breweries. The first recorded brewer in Massachusetts was a man named John W. in 1639, who operated in Cambridge. The brewing practices of these early colonists reflected the methods and styles popular in Europe, particularly those from England, Germany, and the Netherlands. These settlers often brewed ales, which were easier to produce than lagers, as the latter required specific fermentation conditions that were not easily replicated in the early colonial environment.

The colonial period was marked by a diverse range of brewing practices, influenced by the various European cultures that settled in America. For instance, German immigrants brought with them lager brewing techniques, which would later become dominant in the American beer landscape. The British settlers primarily brewed ales, which were characterized by their warm fermentation processes and distinct hop flavors. This blend of brewing traditions created a unique American beer culture that began to take shape.

As the colonies grew, so did the number of breweries. By the 1770s, there were approximately 150 breweries in America, and beer consumption was on the rise. Beer became a staple in the daily lives of many colonists, playing a significant role in social gatherings and community events. The act of brewing beer was often a communal effort, with families and neighbors coming together to share in the production and enjoyment of beer. This social aspect of beer would remain a fundamental characteristic of American brewing culture.

However, the American Revolution had profound impacts on the brewing industry. Many brewers supported the revolutionaries, and beer became a symbol of resistance against British rule. The war disrupted trade routes and supply chains, leading to a scarcity of ingredients, particularly hops and malt. Despite these challenges, breweries adapted by sourcing local ingredients and utilizing alternative methods, ensuring that the tradition of brewing continued.

Following the Revolution, the brewing industry began to stabilize and grow. The establishment of the United States as an independent nation opened new opportunities for breweries, allowing them to expand their markets. The first commercial lager brewery was established in 1840 by German immigrant John Wagner in Philadelphia. This marked a significant turning point as lager gained immense popularity, leading to the creation of iconic American beer styles.

The foundations laid by these early American breweries helped shape the future of beer in the United States. By the mid-19th century, larger commercial breweries began to dominate the market, introducing mass production techniques and paving the way for the global beer industry we know today. The legacy of these first American breweries is evident in the craft beer movement of the late 20th century, which sought to revive traditional brewing methods and celebrate local ingredients.

In conclusion, the first American breweries were more than mere producers of beer; they were integral to the social fabric of early American life. Their adaptability, innovation, and commitment to quality laid the groundwork for a vibrant brewing culture that continues to evolve and thrive in the modern era.

Chapter 7

Beer and Prohibition

The Temperance Movement: Early Calls for Prohibition

The Temperance Movement emerged as a significant social reform initiative in the early 19th century, primarily in the United States and parts of Europe. Rooted in a complex interplay of social, religious, and political factors, the movement sought to reduce or eliminate the consumption of alcohol, with beer being one of the primary targets of its advocacy. The call for temperance was sparked by the belief that alcohol consumption was the source of a myriad of social problems, including crime, poverty, and family disintegration.

Origins and Ideological Underpinnings

The roots of the Temperance Movement can be traced back to the late 18th century, with early advocates promoting moderation in alcohol consumption. However, it wasn't until the 1820s that the movement gained significant traction. Groups like the American Temperance Society, founded in 1826, began to gain prominence by promoting the idea of total abstinence from all alcoholic beverages. This shift reflected a growing belief that moral and social decay was closely linked to alcohol consumption, particularly among the working class and immigrant populations.

Religious groups played a pivotal role in the movement's expansion. Evangelical Protestants, particularly Methodists and Baptists, viewed alcohol as a moral failing and a spiritual poison. They organized revivals and camp meetings, where they preached the virtues of sobriety and the dangers of intoxication. This moral framing resonated with many, leading to a widespread cultural shift against drinking.

Societal Impact and Advocacy

The movement's influence extended beyond religious circles and began to permeate various aspects of society. Social reformers argued that alcohol was responsible for domestic violence, unemployment, and poverty, and they sought legislative measures to curb its consumption. By the 1840s, the movement had escalated, with numerous local and state organizations advocating for laws to restrict or ban the sale of alcohol.

One of the most significant milestones of this period was the establishment of the "cold water army," which promoted the idea of substituting alcohol with water as a means of achieving sobriety. The movement also saw the rise of women's reform groups, who highlighted the detrimental impact of alcohol on family life. Women like Frances Willard, who later became the president of the Women's Christian Temperance Union (WCTU), emphasized the need for women's voices in the temperance debate, arguing that alcohol threatened not only personal well-being but also the sanctity of the home.

Political Mobilization and Early Legislation

As the movement gained momentum, it began to exert political influence. Advocates lobbied for legislation aimed at regulating the production and sale of alcohol. Various states enacted laws restricting alcohol sales, and by the late 19th and early 20th centuries, the movement had garnered enough support to push for a national prohibition.

The culmination of these early efforts was the introduction of the 18th Amendment to the United States Constitution in 1919, which formally prohibited the manufacture, sale, and transportation of intoxicating liquors. This amendment was the result of decades of activism fueled by the temperance movement's ideology, which painted alcohol as a societal ill that needed to be eradicated for the greater good.

Conclusion

The early calls for prohibition set in motion a transformative social movement that would redefine American cultural landscapes and legislative practices regarding alcohol. The Temperance Movement not only reflected deep-seated anxieties about alcohol's role in society but also highlighted the evolving dynamics of gender, class, and morality in the 19th century. Its legacy would resonate throughout the 20th century, ultimately leading to Prohibition, a period that would challenge the very fabric of American life and culture. The historical significance of this movement serves as a lens through which to understand contemporary discussions around alcohol consumption, regulation, and public health.

Prohibition in the United States: 1920–1933

Prohibition, a significant chapter in American history, marked the period from 1920 to 1933 when the production, distribution, and sale of alcoholic beverages were constitutionally outlawed. This period was initiated by the 18th Amendment to the United States Constitution, alongside the Volstead Act, which defined and enforced the terms of prohibition. Rooted in the temperance movement that gained momentum in the late 19th and early 20th centuries, Prohibition aimed to curb the rampant alcohol consumption that many believed was responsible for societal issues, including crime, poverty, and family disintegration.

The temperance movement was driven by various social, religious, and political groups, including the Women's Christian Temperance Union (WCTU) and the Anti-Saloon League. Proponents argued that alcohol was a destructive force undermining public morality and health. Their efforts culminated in the ratification of the 18th Amendment in 1919, which took effect on January 17, 1920. However, the expectation that prohibition would eliminate alcohol consumption proved overly optimistic.

Instead, Prohibition led to unintended consequences that fundamentally altered American society. The demand for alcohol persisted, leading to the rise of illegal production and distribution networks, commonly referred to as speakeasies and bootlegging operations. Organized crime syndicates, most notably led by figures like Al Capone, capitalized on the lucrative black market for alcohol. The law enforcement system struggled to contain the rampant illegal activities, leading to a significant increase in crime rates and corruption among law enforcement officials.

The impact of Prohibition on the beer industry was particularly pronounced. Breweries, unable to produce and sell legal beer, faced financial ruin. Many breweries were forced to close, while others sought alternative products, such as soft drinks or near-beer (a beverage containing less than 0.5% alcohol), to survive. The beer they could produce was often of poor quality, leading to a proliferation of unsafe and unregulated products, further endangering public health.

Public sentiment towards Prohibition gradually shifted as the social ramifications became evident. The initial support from certain segments of society began to erode as the consequences of the ban became apparent. The rise of speakeasies, where people could drink in secret, became a symbol of defiance against the restrictive laws. These underground bars fostered a vibrant culture of jazz music and socializing, contributing to the cultural landscape of the Roaring Twenties.

The economic fallout from Prohibition also played a crucial role in its eventual repeal. The Great Depression, which began in 1929, led to widespread unemployment and economic instability. Many Americans viewed the re-legalization of alcohol as a potential means of economic recovery. The financial burden of enforcing Prohibition, coupled with the loss of tax revenue from the alcohol industry, further fueled calls for its repeal.

In 1933, the 21st Amendment was ratified, effectively ending Prohibition and restoring the legal status of alcohol. The repeal was celebrated as a victory for individual liberties and a recognition of the failure of the prohibitionist policies. The reintegration of beer into American society marked a significant turning point, leading to the resurgence of breweries and the establishment of a more regulated alcohol industry.

In summary, Prohibition in the United States from 1920 to 1933 was a complex period characterized by the clash between moral ideals and the realities of human behavior. While it aimed to eliminate the perceived dangers of alcohol, it instead fostered a culture of lawlessness, significantly impacted the beer industry, and ultimately led to its own undoing. The lessons learned during this tumultuous time continue to influence contemporary discussions about alcohol regulation and public policy.

The Impact of Prohibition on the Beer Industry

Prohibition, enacted in the United States from 1920 to 1933, was one of the most significant and transformative periods in the history of American alcohol consumption, particularly affecting the beer industry. The 18th Amendment and the subsequent Volstead Act made it illegal to manufacture, sell, or transport intoxicating liquors, which fundamentally altered the landscape of brewing and consumption in the nation.

Initially, Prohibition had a catastrophic effect on the beer industry, which had become a staple of American social life and economy. Before Prohibition, there were thousands of breweries operating across the country, employing hundreds of thousands of workers and contributing significantly to local economies. The sudden ban on alcohol production led to the closure of approximately 1,200 breweries, with many being forced to shut their doors permanently. The loss of jobs was staggering, with an estimated 400,000 workers left unemployed, not to mention the ripple effects on industries dependent on brewing, such as agriculture, transportation, and retail.

As breweries closed, many former brewers sought alternative avenues for survival. A number of them adapted their competencies to produce non-alcoholic products, such as malted beverages, soft drinks, and even ice cream. However, the drastic changes led to a loss of expertise and innovation in brewing techniques that would take decades to recover. Moreover, the few breweries that remained operational often diverted their production to near-beer (a low-alcohol beverage) or other legal alternatives, which significantly impacted the quality and variety of beer available to consumers.

Prohibition also gave rise to the underground market for beer, leading to the proliferation of bootlegging and speakeasies. Organized crime seized the opportunity to fill the void left by legal breweries, smuggling alcohol across borders and operating illicit establishments where beer was served. This black market not only undermined the legal economy but also contributed to a rise in violence and corruption. Breweries that had previously operated in the open now had to navigate a dangerous underworld, often resorting to bribery and collusion with law enforcement.

Additionally, Prohibition changed the cultural perception of alcohol. Beer, once seen as a communal drink enjoyed in social settings, became associated with crime and illicit activities. This shift altered public attitudes toward drinking and contributed to a stigma surrounding beer that persisted even after the repeal of Prohibition. The narrative of beer as a benign social lubricant was overshadowed by the image of it being part of the underground scene, complicating the return of breweries to the mainstream market post-Prohibition.

When the 21st Amendment repealed Prohibition in 1933, the beer industry faced new challenges. Many breweries had closed permanently or been absorbed into larger corporations, and the landscape of beer production had changed. The remaining breweries were often smaller and less competitive, struggling to regain their market share in an industry now dominated by a few large players. The return to brewing meant not only re-establishing production but also rebuilding consumer trust and interest in beer as a legitimate beverage choice.

In conclusion, the impact of Prohibition on the beer industry was profound and multifaceted. It led to the closure of countless breweries, the rise of illegal markets, a shift in cultural perceptions of alcohol, and a long road to recovery post-repeal. The legacy of this era is still felt in the contemporary beer culture of the United States, influencing everything from brewing practices to consumer attitudes toward alcohol. The lessons learned from this tumultuous period continue to shape the regulatory landscape and the dynamics of the alcohol industry today.

Bootlegging and Speakeasies: Beer in the Underground Market

The era of Prohibition in the United States (1920-1933) was marked by a dramatic shift in the landscape of alcohol consumption, leading to the emergence of a vibrant underground market for beer and other alcoholic beverages. The 18th Amendment, ratified in 1919, prohibited the manufacture, sale, and transportation of intoxicating liquors, a move that aimed to curb alcohol consumption in light of public health concerns and social issues tied to drinking. Instead of eliminating the demand for alcohol, Prohibition inadvertently spurred a thriving black market, giving rise to bootlegging and speakeasies.

Bootlegging: The Art of Illicit Trade

Bootlegging refers to the illegal production and distribution of alcohol during Prohibition. While the term originally described the concealment of flasks in the legs of boots, it evolved to encompass a broader range of illicit activities. Bootleggers operated in secrecy, smuggling beer from Canada or distilling it in hidden stills. The production often took place in basements, garages, or abandoned warehouses, with makeshift breweries using whatever materials were available. The quality of the beer varied widely; some bootleggers produced potent brews that were harsh and potentially dangerous, while others focused on creating more palatable products to meet customer demands.

The underground market necessitated a network of distribution channels. Smugglers, often referred to as "rum-runners," would transport alcohol across state lines or into urban centers. Corruption among law enforcement officials and local governments was rampant, as many were bribed to turn a blind eye to illegal activities. This environment fostered the growth of organized crime, with notorious figures like Al Capone capitalizing on the lucrative beer trade. The profitability of bootlegging was staggering—at its peak, it is estimated that organized crime made hundreds of millions of dollars from illegal alcohol sales.

Speakeasies: The Secret Bars of the Roaring Twenties
Parallel to the rise of bootlegging was the emergence of speakeasies—underground bars that served illicit drinks, including beer. The name "speakeasy" is believed to have originated from patrons speaking quietly or "easily" to avoid drawing attention to these secret venues. Speakeasies could be found in basements, back rooms, and even private homes, often disguised as soda shops or legitimate businesses.

Entry into a speakeasy typically required a password, which added an element of exclusivity and intrigue. Inside, patrons enjoyed not only beer but also a variety of cocktails, often mixed with homemade spirits. The ambiance was lively, characterized by jazz music, dancing, and social interaction, making these venues popular among the youth and the cultural elite. The speakeasy phenomenon played a crucial role in the social fabric of the 1920s, providing a space for people to gather, celebrate, and express themselves freely in a time of repression.

Cultural Impact and Legacy
The underground market for beer during Prohibition had a lasting cultural impact on American society. It challenged the notion of legality, as many citizens openly defied the law by seeking out speakeasies and engaging with bootleggers. This era also marked the genesis of some of America's most enduring drinking traditions and cocktail culture.

Moreover, the defiance of Prohibition laid the groundwork for changing societal attitudes toward alcohol. When Prohibition was repealed in 1933, the beer industry was quick to re-establish itself legally, capitalizing on the burgeoning demand for alcohol. The innovations and practices developed during the underground market period would influence the brewing industry for decades to come, leading to the diverse and rich beer culture we know today.

In summary, the era of bootlegging and speakeasies during Prohibition represents a fascinating chapter in the history of beer, characterized by resilience, creativity, and a spirit of rebellion against restrictive laws. Through illicit trade and clandestine socializing, the public found ways to maintain a vibrant drinking culture, which ultimately contributed to the evolution of beer in American society.

The Repeal of Prohibition: The Return of Legal Beer

The history of beer in the United States is deeply intertwined with the era of Prohibition, which lasted from 1920 to 1933. This period was marked by the 18th Amendment to the Constitution, which outlawed the manufacture, sale, and transportation of intoxicating liquors. Prohibition was largely a result of the temperance movement, which had gained momentum in the late 19th and early 20th centuries, driven by a mix of social, political, and religious factors. Advocates believed that banning alcohol would reduce crime, corruption, and social problems, but the reality proved far more complex.

As soon as Prohibition took effect on January 17, 1920, the beer industry faced an existential crisis. Breweries, large and small, were forced to shut down or pivot to alternative products. Many breweries attempted to survive by producing non-alcoholic beverages such as soft drinks or "near beers" (beers containing less than 0.5% alcohol by volume). However, these products were often unsatisfactory to consumers craving the taste and effects of traditional beer, leading to a surge in illegal activities.

With the ban on legal alcohol sales, a thriving underground economy emerged, characterized by bootlegging and speakeasies—illegal bars that operated in secrecy. Organized crime syndicates stepped in to fill the void left by legal breweries, leading to increased violence and corruption. The public's appetite for beer only intensified, and the hypocrisy of Prohibition became apparent as law enforcement struggled to control illegal production and consumption.

As the 1920s progressed, the negative consequences of Prohibition began to mount. The economic impact was significant; breweries that had once employed thousands of workers faced closure, while government tax revenues from alcohol sales plummeted. The economic devastation of the Great Depression further exacerbated the situation, leading many to reassess the prohibitionist stance. Taxing and regulating alcohol seemed a more viable solution to the economic malaise, particularly as the government sought new sources of revenue.

By the early 1930s, public sentiment began to shift. The growing recognition of the failure of Prohibition was accompanied by increasing calls for its repeal. In 1933, the political landscape saw a significant change with the election of Franklin D. Roosevelt, who campaigned on a platform that included the repeal of Prohibition. On December 5, 1933, the 21st Amendment was ratified, officially ending Prohibition and allowing the legal production and sale of alcohol to resume.

The repeal of Prohibition marked a watershed moment for the beer industry in the United States. Breweries reopened their doors, and many new breweries emerged, eager to capitalize on the pent-up demand for legal beer. The return of legal beer not only revitalized the industry but also sparked a cultural renaissance around beer consumption. Beer became a symbol of American freedom and a tool for socializing in post-Prohibition society.

As legal beer returned to the market, key changes in consumer preferences and brewing practices began to emerge. The rise of brands like Anheuser-Busch and Miller highlighted a shift toward mass production, but it also set the stage for future craft movements. The diversity of beer styles and flavors would eventually flourish, leading to the burgeoning craft beer scene that emerged in the late 20th century.

In conclusion, the repeal of Prohibition was not just a return to legal beer; it was a pivotal moment that reshaped American society, culture, and the brewing industry. It underscored the complex relationship between beer and American identity, highlighting how deeply embedded alcohol is in social practices, economic structures, and political landscapes. The legacy of this era continues to influence the brewing industry and beer culture to this day.

Chapter 8

The Globalization of Beer

The Expansion of Beer into Asia and Africa

The globalization of beer has seen a remarkable trajectory, particularly in its expansion into Asia and Africa, where traditional and contemporary brewing practices are evolving and intertwining with local cultures. This section explores the historical context, cultural significance, and recent developments in the beer industries of these two diverse continents.

Historical Context

Historically, beer has been a staple beverage in various forms across the world, but its presence in Asia and Africa has been closely tied to the cultural practices and local resources of the regions. In Asia, traditional fermented beverages have existed for millennia, such as sake in Japan and chang in Thailand, which, while different from Western beer, share fermentation processes and ingredients like grains. The introduction of European brewing techniques and lager styles during the colonial period significantly influenced the local beer culture.

In Africa, indigenous brewing practices have also been prevalent, particularly in sub-Saharan regions where local grains like sorghum and millet are used to create traditional beers, such as chibuku in Zimbabwe and mbede in Nigeria. However, with the colonial encounter, European brewing methods began to penetrate African societies, leading to the establishment of breweries that produced lagers tailored to local tastes.

Cultural Significance

The cultural significance of beer in both Asia and Africa cannot be overstated. In many African communities, beer is more than a beverage; it plays a central role in social rituals, celebrations, and communal gatherings. Traditional brews are often served during ceremonies, weddings, and festivals, embodying a sense of community and cultural identity.

In Asia, beer has also become a significant part of social life, particularly in urban areas where globalization has led to the rise of beer consumption among younger generations. Countries like China and India are witnessing a burgeoning craft beer scene, with local breweries experimenting with unique flavors that blend traditional ingredients with contemporary brewing techniques.

Recent Developments

The last few decades have seen a remarkable growth in the beer market across Asia and Africa. In Asia, countries like China have become one of the largest beer markets in the world, driven by increasing disposable incomes and changing consumer preferences. The emergence of craft breweries in urban centers has transformed the beer landscape, with local brewers drawing inspiration from both Western styles and traditional Asian ingredients, such as rice, ginger, and jasmine.

India is also experiencing a craft beer revolution, with microbreweries popping up in major cities like Bangalore and Mumbai. These establishments cater to a growing population of young professionals seeking innovative and diverse beer options, often incorporating local flavors into their offerings.

In Africa, the beer market is expanding rapidly, with multinational corporations establishing breweries to tap into the growing demand. The craft beer movement is also gaining momentum, with an increasing number of small breweries focusing on quality and local sourcing. Countries like South Africa are leading the charge, with a vibrant craft beer scene that emphasizes unique flavors and traditional brewing methods.

Challenges and Opportunities

Despite the growth potential, the expansion of beer in Asia and Africa faces challenges. Regulatory environments can be complex, and cultural attitudes towards alcohol consumption vary significantly across regions. In some areas, traditional norms may discourage alcohol consumption, while in others, new social trends are emerging that embrace beer as part of modern life.

However, the opportunities for the beer industry in these continents are immense. With a young, urbanizing population and a growing interest in craft and premium products, breweries that can authentically integrate local culture and flavors into their offerings are poised for success.

In conclusion, the expansion of beer into Asia and Africa reflects not only the globalization of a beloved beverage but also the dynamic interplay between tradition and modernity. As local breweries continue to flourish and innovate, beer's role in these regions will likely evolve further, enriching both local cultures and the global beer narrative.

European Beer Traditions in the Americas

The story of beer in the Americas is deeply intertwined with the migration patterns and cultural exchanges of European settlers who brought their brewing traditions across the Atlantic. From the early colonial period to the modern era, European beer styles, brewing techniques, and cultural practices significantly influenced the development of the American beer landscape.

Early Settlements and European Influence

When European settlers arrived in North America, beer was already a vital part of their daily lives. The English, Dutch, Germans, and other nationalities brought their brewing knowledge with them, establishing the foundation for the American beer culture. In the early 1600s, the first English colonists in Jamestown and Plymouth brewed beer using the ingredients available to them, primarily barley and corn. The harsh conditions of the New World, combined with the settlers' desire for familiar comforts, led to the rapid adoption of brewing practices.

The Dutch, particularly in New Amsterdam (now New York City), introduced their unique beer styles. They brought with them the tradition of brewing ales and porters, which became popular among the diverse population. This blending of European traditions with native ingredients marked the beginning of a distinct American beer identity.

The German Influence

One of the most significant influences on American beer came from German immigrants in the 19th century. As they settled in areas such as Wisconsin, Missouri, and Pennsylvania, they introduced lager brewing, which was a relatively new style at the time. Lagers, known for their smooth, crisp taste, quickly gained popularity, leading to the establishment of numerous breweries across the Midwest.

The German influence also extended to beer culture and social practices. Beer gardens, which were a staple of German social life, began to appear in American cities, providing a communal space for people to gather, enjoy beer, and socialize. Events such as Oktoberfest, which celebrate German beer culture, have been embraced and adapted into American traditions, fostering a sense of community and cultural exchange.

The Role of British and Belgian Traditions

In addition to German influences, British brewing traditions have played a crucial role in shaping American beer styles. British ales, particularly pale ales, stouts, and porters, became popular among American brewers and drinkers. The establishment of the first commercial brewery in the United States in 1632, the New Amsterdam Brewery, showcased British brewing techniques, setting the stage for the rise of ale production in America.

Belgian beer traditions also found a foothold in the American beer landscape. The unique characteristics of Belgian ales, including fruity esters and complex flavors, intrigued American brewers. In the late 20th century, the craft beer movement sparked a renewed interest in these styles, leading to the emergence of breweries that focused on Belgian-inspired beers. This cross-pollination of brewing styles has resulted in the creation of hybrid American beers that reflect both traditional Belgian methods and contemporary American tastes.

Modern American Craft Beer Scene
The craft beer revolution of the late 20th and early 21st centuries has further transformed the relationship between European beer traditions and American brewing. Craft breweries have embraced the rich tapestry of European styles while infusing them with local ingredients and innovative brewing techniques. This has led to the emergence of diverse beer styles, including IPAs, sours, and barrel-aged stouts, that draw inspiration from European heritage while carving out a unique American identity.

Today, beer festivals celebrating European traditions are common across the United States, showcasing the influence of European brewing heritage on the modern craft beer scene. Events like the Great American Beer Festival highlight the diversity and creativity of American brewers, who continue to honor their European roots while pushing the boundaries of what beer can be.

In conclusion, the European beer traditions brought to the Americas have had a lasting impact on the evolution of beer culture in the region. From early colonial brews to the craft beer movement, the interplay of European styles and American innovation has created a vibrant and dynamic beer landscape that celebrates both heritage and creativity.

The Growth of Multinational Brewing Corporations
The landscape of the beer industry has undergone a significant transformation over the past few decades, with the rise of multinational brewing corporations (MBCs) emerging as a defining feature of global commerce in beer. This growth has been driven by several interrelated factors, including globalization, technological advancements, shifts in consumer preferences, and strategic mergers and acquisitions.

Globalization and Market Expansion
The phenomenon of globalization has facilitated the expansion of beer markets beyond local and national boundaries. As economies around the world became increasingly interconnected, MBCs seized the opportunity to penetrate new markets, particularly in developing regions. Countries in Asia, Africa, and Latin America presented untapped potential for growth, where rising disposable incomes and changing consumer habits created a burgeoning demand for beer. MBCs

effectively leveraged their established brands, marketing expertise, and distribution networks to introduce their products to these new consumer bases.

Technological Advancements

Advances in technology have played a pivotal role in the growth of MBCs. Innovations in brewing technology have enabled large-scale production while maintaining quality and consistency across different regions. Automated brewing systems, advanced fermentation techniques, and improved quality control measures have allowed MBCs to produce beer more efficiently and cost-effectively. Additionally, developments in packaging and distribution, such as the use of refrigerated transport and sophisticated supply chain logistics, have streamlined the process of getting beer from breweries to consumers worldwide.

Consumer Preferences and Craft Beer Trends

The rise of craft beer in the late 20th century marked a significant shift in consumer preferences, with many consumers seeking unique flavors, artisanal quality, and local authenticity over mass-produced options. In response to this trend, MBCs adopted various strategies to capture the burgeoning craft beer market. Many corporations established their own craft beer brands or acquired successful craft breweries to diversify their offerings. This allowed MBCs to cater to the evolving tastes of consumers while maintaining their core product lines.

Mergers and Acquisitions

The growth of multinational brewing corporations has been significantly propelled by strategic mergers and acquisitions. The beer industry has witnessed a wave of consolidation, with major players acquiring both domestic and international breweries to expand their portfolios and gain competitive advantages. For instance, the merger of Anheuser-Busch and InBev in 2008 created one of the world's largest brewing companies, effectively reshaping the global beer market. Such mergers not only increase market share but also enhance operational efficiencies and economies of scale, enabling MBCs to dominate the marketplace.

Challenges and Criticisms

While the growth of MBCs has led to increased availability and variety of beer, it has also triggered criticisms regarding the homogenization of beer culture. Critics argue that the dominance of MBCs can stifle local breweries and diminish the diversity of offerings, as smaller breweries struggle to compete against the marketing power and distribution capabilities of their larger counterparts. Furthermore, concerns have been raised about the impact of MBCs on traditional brewing practices and regional beer styles.

Conclusion
The growth of multinational brewing corporations has fundamentally altered the beer industry, creating a complex interplay between local traditions and global commerce. As MBCs continue to expand their reach and influence, they face the dual challenge of meeting the diverse preferences of consumers while navigating the cultural implications of their dominance. The future of the beer industry will likely involve a delicate balance between the global strategies of MBCs and the resilience of local breweries, fostering a vibrant and diverse beer landscape that honors both innovation and tradition.

Beer Tourism: Festivals, Breweries, and Tasting Events
Beer tourism has emerged as a vibrant and dynamic sector within the broader travel industry, attracting enthusiasts and casual drinkers alike to explore the rich tapestry of beer culture across the globe. This phenomenon encompasses a wide range of activities, including visits to breweries, participation in beer festivals, and attendance at tasting events, all of which allow travelers to immerse themselves in local brewing traditions, innovative craft brews, and the social aspects surrounding beer consumption.

Festivals: Celebrating the Craft
Beer festivals are one of the most recognizable aspects of beer tourism, drawing thousands of attendees from near and far. These events often showcase a plethora of breweries, ranging from large multinational corporations to small, independent craft brewers. Notable examples include the Great American Beer Festival in Denver, Colorado, and Oktoberfest in Munich, Germany, which are both renowned for their scale and diversity. At these festivals, visitors have the opportunity to taste a wide array of beer styles—from IPAs to stouts—and engage with brewers who are passionate about their craft.

Festivals often go beyond just beer tasting; they also feature live music, food pairings, and educational seminars. These interactive elements foster a sense of community and celebration, allowing attendees to not only enjoy the beverage but also learn about its production, history, and the intricate processes involved in brewing. Such events are an excellent way for local economies to benefit, as they draw tourists who spend on accommodations, food, and entertainment.

Breweries: The Heart of Beer Culture
Visiting breweries is another cornerstone of beer tourism. Many travelers seek out brewery tours as they provide a behind-the-scenes look at the brewing process. These tours typically cover the history of the brewery, the ingredients used, and the unique brewing methods

employed. Visitors can often sample fresh beer straight from the source, which provides an unparalleled tasting experience.

Some breweries have established themselves as destinations, offering comprehensive visitor experiences that may include taprooms, restaurants, and even gift shops. The rise of craft breweries has led to a boom in brewery tourism, with regions like the Pacific Northwest and New England becoming popular hotspots. In these locations, brewery trails—collections of breweries within a geographical area—have been developed, making it easier for tourists to explore multiple venues in one trip.

Tasting Events: The Art of Appreciation
Tasting events are another vital element of beer tourism, allowing attendees to deepen their appreciation for the nuances of various beer styles. These events can range from informal gatherings at local pubs to sophisticated tastings hosted by breweries or beer clubs. During these tastings, experienced guides may educate participants on pairing beer with food, highlighting how different flavors can complement or contrast with one another.

Special events such as "beer and food pairing dinners" can elevate the tasting experience, showcasing the versatility of beer in gastronomy. Chefs and brewers often collaborate to create multi-course meals that highlight specific beer styles, enhancing the overall culinary experience. Additionally, many regions host seasonal beer tastings that celebrate local ingredients, seasonal brews, or specific beer styles, adding a unique touch to the tasting experience.

The Economic Impact of Beer Tourism
The impact of beer tourism on local economies cannot be overstated. It generates significant revenue through direct spending on accommodations, food, and merchandise, while also creating jobs in the hospitality and tourism sectors. Moreover, beer tourism has prompted the development of local infrastructure, including hotels, restaurants, and transportation services tailored to cater to the needs of beer tourists.

In conclusion, beer tourism encapsulates a rich cultural experience that combines the appreciation of brewing artistry with social interaction and community engagement. Whether through festivals, brewery visits, or tasting events, beer tourism invites enthusiasts to explore the diverse world of beer, fostering a deeper understanding and appreciation of this ancient beverage while simultaneously contributing to the local and global economy.

Beer and Global Trade: Exporting Beer Across Continents

The global beer industry has evolved significantly over the centuries, transitioning from localized brewing practices to a vast, interconnected market that spans continents. As beer became a staple beverage in various cultures, its exportation emerged as a vital component of the global trade economy. This section delves into the historical and contemporary dynamics of beer exportation, highlighting its economic, cultural, and social implications.

Historical Context

The global beer trade can trace its roots back to ancient civilizations, where the exchange of beer and brewing knowledge crossed borders. Early evidence of beer production and trade has been documented in Mesopotamia and Egypt, where beer was not only a dietary staple but also a commodity traded along with other goods. As civilizations expanded, so did the reach of beer, with trade routes facilitating the exchange of brewing techniques and ingredients. The medieval period saw further developments, particularly in Europe, where brewing guilds began to standardize production methods, leading to the establishment of regional beer styles that were traded across borders.

Colonial Expansion and Beer Trade

With the age of exploration and colonialism in the 15th and 16th centuries, European powers such as Britain, Spain, and the Netherlands established colonies around the world. This era marked a significant increase in the exportation of beer, particularly to North America and the Caribbean. British settlers brought their brewing traditions with them, laying the foundation for the American beer industry. The trade was not merely one-sided; colonies also produced unique beer styles that were exported back to Europe, showcasing the reciprocal nature of beer trade.

Industrialization and Global Commerce

The Industrial Revolution in the 18th and 19th centuries revolutionized brewing processes and increased production capacities. This period saw the rise of large-scale breweries capable of producing beer in massive quantities, making it feasible to export beer internationally. Advances in transportation, including the advent of railroads and steamships, further facilitated the movement of beer across continents. As a result, iconic European beer brands began to dominate international markets, establishing a global presence that continues to this day.

Contemporary Global Beer Trade

In the modern era, the globalization of beer has taken on new dimensions, driven by the rise of multinational corporations and the craft beer movement. Major global players like Anheuser-Busch InBev and Heineken have expanded their reach through acquisitions and partnerships, leading to a diverse portfolio of beer brands available worldwide. This has enabled breweries to leverage economies of scale, streamlining production and distribution processes to meet global demand.

Conversely, the craft beer movement has emerged as a response to industrialization, prioritizing quality, local ingredients, and unique flavors. Craft breweries have gained traction not only in their home countries but also in international markets. The export of craft beer has become a burgeoning segment of the industry, with breweries seeking to establish their identities abroad and participate in global beer festivals.

Cultural Exchange and Societal Impact
The global trade of beer has transcended mere economic transactions; it has fostered cultural exchange and social connections. Beer festivals and tasting events around the world celebrate diverse brewing traditions, allowing consumers to experience flavors from different cultures. This exchange has also influenced brewing practices, leading to hybrid styles that reflect the melding of global brewing techniques and local tastes.

Moreover, the exportation of beer contributes significantly to local economies, creating jobs in brewing, distribution, and hospitality sectors. As beer becomes a symbol of social gatherings, its role in fostering community bonds cannot be understated. From local pubs to international beer festivals, the shared experience of enjoying a beer facilitates connections among individuals from varied backgrounds.

In conclusion, the exportation of beer across continents is a multifaceted phenomenon that intertwines history, commerce, and culture. As the global beer market continues to evolve, understanding the dynamics of beer trade will remain essential in appreciating its role in shaping societies and economies around the world.

Chapter 9

Beer and Politics

Beer Taxes: Historical and Modern Examples

Beer, one of the oldest fermented beverages known to humanity, has long been associated with social gatherings, rituals, and economies. However, it has also been closely tied to taxation, a practice dating back to ancient civilizations where governments sought to regulate and profit from the production and consumption of alcohol. The history of beer taxes reflects broader socio-political contexts, economic strategies, and cultural attitudes toward alcohol consumption.

Historical Context

In ancient Mesopotamia, beer was a staple in daily life, and its production was often linked to temple offerings and state-sponsored activities. The Code of Hammurabi, dating back to around 1754 BCE, included regulations on beer sales and prices, indicating that the state recognized the need to control this vital commodity. Sumerians even had a goddess of beer, Ninkasi, whose hymns included recipes and methods of brewing, underscoring the beverage's importance in their culture.

As societies evolved, so did the imposition of beer taxes. In medieval Europe, monarchs began taxing ale and beer as a means to generate revenue. For instance, King Henry II of England instituted the "Beer Tax" in the 12th century, which mandated payments for the right to brew and sell beer. This tax was often met with resistance from local populations, leading to riots and protests, highlighting the contentious relationship between taxation and public sentiment.

The Modern Era

The 20th century saw significant developments in beer taxation, particularly in the wake of the Prohibition era in the United States (1920–1933). The repeal of Prohibition in 1933 led to the introduction of various taxes, including excise taxes on beer, which became a crucial source of government revenue. These taxes were established not only to regulate the industry but also to discourage excessive consumption by imposing financial burdens on producers and consumers alike.

Today, beer taxes in many countries serve multiple purposes, including revenue generation for government programs, public health initiatives, and social policies aimed at reducing alcohol-related harm. For example, in the United States, federal excise taxes on beer vary based on production volumes, with small breweries benefiting from lower rates to promote local industry growth. State and local governments also impose their own taxes, leading to a complex web of taxation that can significantly affect beer prices.

Comparative Global Examples
Globally, the approach to beer taxation varies widely. In the United Kingdom, the Beer Duty is levied based on the alcohol content of the beer, with higher rates applied to stronger brews. This system has faced criticism from brewers who argue that it disproportionately affects small craft breweries compared to larger multinational corporations, which can better absorb such costs.

Conversely, Germany's Reinheitsgebot (Beer Purity Law) has influenced its tax structure and beer culture. The country's beer tax is relatively low compared to other European nations, promoting its rich brewing tradition. Germany's Oktoberfest, one of the world's largest beer festivals, benefits both from lower taxation and the cultural significance attached to beer, further solidifying its status as a national beverage.

In countries like Denmark and Norway, high beer taxes are implemented as part of broader public health strategies aimed at reducing alcohol consumption. These taxes can lead to significant price increases, resulting in cross-border shopping as consumers seek more affordable options in neighboring countries with lower taxes.

Conclusion
The taxation of beer has evolved from ancient regulations in Mesopotamia to complex modern systems that reflect societal values and economic priorities. While taxes on beer can generate substantial government revenue, they also provoke debates about public health, industry sustainability, and cultural heritage. As global attitudes toward alcohol continue to change, so too will the frameworks governing beer taxation, highlighting the ongoing interplay between economics, society, and this ancient beverage.

Beer as a Political Tool: Public Houses and Revolutions

The intersection of beer and politics is a fascinating narrative woven into the fabric of human history, revealing how this beloved beverage has functioned as a vehicle for social change and political expression. Public houses, or pubs, have long served not only as places for social interaction but also as critical venues for political discourse, mobilization, and even revolution.

Public houses have historically been the gathering spots where individuals from various walks of life could congregate to share news, ideas, and grievances. In societies where the press was limited or censored, these establishments often became the epicenters of critical political discussions. Alehouses and taverns provided a space where patrons could openly debate social issues, share revolutionary ideas, and organize collective actions against oppressive regimes. The convivial atmosphere fostered by beer drinking created an environment conducive to camaraderie and solidarity, which proved essential during times of political upheaval.

One of the most notable examples of beer's role in political activism is found in 18th-century England. The pub culture of the time was deeply intertwined with the political climate, particularly during the lead-up to the English Civil War and the Glorious Revolution. Public houses became crucibles for political thought, where ordinary citizens could discuss the implications of monarchy, taxation, and the rights of individuals. The phrase "no taxation without representation" became a rallying cry during this era, and many of the discussions that birthed this sentiment occurred over pints of ale in local taverns.

The American Revolution provides another compelling illustration of beer's political significance. In the years leading up to independence, colonial pubs were vital in disseminating revolutionary ideas. The Sons of Liberty, a group of patriots opposed to British rule, frequently met in public houses to strategize and coordinate protests against the Stamp Act and other forms of taxation. As revolution brewed, beer served as both a literal and figurative lubricant, facilitating conversations that would lead to a radical rethinking of governance and societal structure.

Moreover, the role of beer in public houses is not limited to mere discussion; it has also served as a tool for protest. During the French Revolution, for example, taverns played a significant role in mobilizing citizens against the monarchy. The consumption of beer became an act of defiance, and public houses were transformed into hubs for revolutionary fervor. The famous phrase "Liberté, égalité, fraternité" was often toasted in these establishments, symbolizing unity and collective purpose among the people.

In addition to their role in revolutionary movements, public houses have historically been used as venues for political campaigns and rallies. Candidates often relied on the informal setting of a pub to connect with voters, deliver speeches, and promote their platforms. Beer, with its ability to lower inhibitions and foster conviviality, has played an instrumental role in creating an approachable atmosphere for political dialogue.

However, the relationship between beer and politics is not solely celebratory; it also reflects the darker side of governance. Governments have historically imposed taxes on beer as a means of revenue generation, which has sometimes led to public unrest. High beer taxes have incited protests, highlighting the beverage's significance in daily life and its role as a barometer of public sentiment.

In conclusion, beer has served as a powerful political tool throughout history, particularly within the social framework of public houses. These gathering places have facilitated revolutionary discourse, mobilized individuals for collective action, and fostered political engagement. As both a symbol of social unity and a catalyst for political change, beer's role in shaping societies is a testament to its enduring influence in the political arena.

The Impact of War on Beer Production and Consumption

War has historically had a profound influence on various aspects of society, and beer production and consumption are no exceptions. The relationship between conflict and brewing can be traced through time, revealing how wars affected not just the availability of beer, but also its cultural significance, production practices, and consumption patterns.

Disruption of Supply Chains

One of the most immediate impacts of war on beer production is the disruption of supply chains. Wars often lead to shortages of key ingredients such as barley, hops, and yeast. For instance, during World War I, the British government implemented strict rationing measures, which included limiting the amount of barley that could be used for brewing. This led to a decline in beer quality and quantity, as brewers were forced to substitute traditional ingredients with less desirable alternatives. The scarcity of resources forced many breweries to innovate, leading to the creation of new styles of beer that relied on whatever grains were available, such as corn or rice.

Changes in Brewing Practices

The impact of war extended beyond ingredient shortages; it also prompted significant changes in brewing practices. During World War II, the United States faced severe material shortages, which affected not just beer but many industries. Breweries adapted by employing creative measures to cope with the wartime economy. For instance, in response to the scarcity of glass, many brewers shifted to aluminum cans, which ultimately contributed to the growth of canned beer as a popular format in the post-war era.

Additionally, some breweries repurposed their facilities for the war effort. Many brewing companies transitioned to producing non-alcoholic beverages or even munitions, which further altered the landscape of availability and consumption during wartime. The introduction of low-alcohol beers was another response to wartime constraints, reflecting both government regulations and consumer demand for beverages suitable for wartime rationing.

Changes in Consumption Patterns
War also affects the social dynamics surrounding beer consumption. During times of conflict, beer often serves as a symbol of camaraderie and resilience. Soldiers and civilians alike frequently turned to beer as a means of coping with the stresses of war. Pubs and taverns became vital social hubs where people gathered to share stories, celebrate small victories, and find solace amid the chaos. The consumption of beer during wartime can foster a sense of community and shared experience, providing an emotional outlet and a temporary escape from the harsh realities of conflict.

Conversely, wartime conditions can also lead to a decline in beer consumption. In some instances, governments have restricted the sale of alcohol during conflicts to maintain public order and productivity. For example, during World War I, many countries implemented prohibition measures to conserve resources for the war effort, leading to a marked decline in brewery production and the consumption of beer.

Post-War Boom
The end of conflicts often heralds a resurgence in beer culture. After World War II, for example, returning soldiers contributed to a boom in beer consumption, as they sought to reclaim a sense of normalcy. Breweries that had survived the war quickly ramped up production to meet the pent-up demand for beer. This post-war era saw the emergence of new beer styles and brands, as breweries sought to capitalize on a newly invigorated market.

Moreover, the experiences of war can lead to the increased popularity of specific beer brands that resonate with national pride or nostalgia. Nationalistic sentiments often translate into a preference for local brews, which can help revive struggling breweries in post-conflict economies.

In conclusion, the impact of war on beer production and consumption is multifaceted, encompassing ingredient shortages, changes in brewing practices, alterations in social dynamics, and eventual booms in the post-war period. Beer has not only survived the trials of war but has also played a crucial role in shaping social interactions and cultural identity during some of humanity's most challenging times.

Government Regulation of Beer in Different Countries
Government regulation of beer varies significantly across the globe, influenced by cultural, historical, economic, and religious factors. As an essential beverage with a long history, beer has often been subject to various forms of oversight, from production and distribution to advertising

and consumption. Understanding these regulations provides insight into how beer is integrated into societies and economies worldwide.

Licensing and Production Regulations

In many countries, brewing beer requires licenses that ensure compliance with health and safety standards. For example, in the United States, the Alcohol and Tobacco Tax and Trade Bureau (TTB) regulates the production of beer at the federal level. Breweries must obtain a Brewer's Notice to legally manufacture beer, which involves extensive paperwork, background checks, and adherence to regulations concerning labeling, advertising, and record-keeping. Similar licensing systems exist in countries such as Canada and Australia, where breweries must comply with both federal and provincial or state regulations.

In contrast, some countries have more relaxed regulations. For instance, several European nations have a long tradition of small-scale brewing, and local governments may have fewer restrictions on artisanal producers. In Belgium, many small breweries operate under a "brewpub" model, where local laws encourage community engagement and local consumption without the stringent oversight seen in larger commercial breweries.

Taxation and Economic Policies

Taxation is a critical aspect of beer regulation that varies widely. In Germany, the Reinheitsgebot or "beer purity law" has historically influenced production methods, but taxation policies have also played a significant role in shaping the beer market. The country imposes a relatively low excise tax on beer compared to spirits, fostering a vibrant brewing culture. This fiscal approach encourages consumption while contributing to the economy through job creation and tourism.

Conversely, some nations impose high taxes on alcohol, including beer, as a means of discouraging consumption for public health reasons. For example, Scandinavian countries such as Sweden and Norway have some of the highest alcohol taxes globally, significantly impacting beer prices and consumption patterns. These high costs often lead to a thriving black market for beer and other alcoholic beverages, as consumers seek cheaper alternatives.

Cultural and Religious Influences

Cultural and religious beliefs also significantly shape beer regulations. In predominantly Muslim countries, such as Saudi Arabia and Iran, alcohol consumption is heavily restricted or outright banned due to Islamic laws. In these countries, beer is either illegal or available only in specific contexts, such as private clubs for non-Muslims. This prohibition not only affects the availability of beer but also influences the brewing culture, resulting in a minimal local beer industry.

Conversely, countries with strong beer traditions, such as the Czech Republic and Germany, celebrate beer as a social lubricant and a cultural artifact. Festivals, such as Oktoberfest, are state-sanctioned events that promote local brewing industries and tourism, reflecting a positive regulatory environment that encourages beer production and consumption.

Advertising and Marketing Regulations

Advertising regulations also vary significantly. In the United States, the TTB oversees advertising practices to ensure that they are not misleading and that they comply with standards set forth in the Federal Alcohol Administration Act. In contrast, some countries have stricter advertising laws, prohibiting advertisements that target children or promote irresponsible drinking behaviors. For instance, in France, regulations restrict alcohol advertising in certain media, emphasizing responsible consumption.

In summary, the regulation of beer differs widely across countries, shaped by a complex interplay of licensing, taxation, cultural norms, and advertising practices. These regulations reflect broader societal attitudes towards alcohol, highlighting the importance of understanding local contexts in the global beer landscape. As beer continues to evolve, the regulatory frameworks will likely adapt, balancing public health concerns with the economic benefits of a thriving brewing industry.

Beer and Diplomacy: How Beer Is Used in International Relations

Beer has long transcended its role as merely a beverage, evolving into a multifaceted symbol that can foster social connections, cultural exchanges, and even diplomatic relationships. The use of beer in international relations is a fascinating aspect of how this ancient drink has woven itself into the fabric of human interaction on a global scale.

Historically, beer has served as a social lubricant, facilitating conversations and negotiations. The act of sharing a drink is often seen as a gesture of goodwill and camaraderie, breaking down barriers that might exist between individuals from different cultures or nations. In diplomatic contexts, sharing beer can soften formal interactions, allowing for a more relaxed atmosphere where candid discussions can take place. This informality can lead to more genuine exchanges and help build rapport between diplomats, fostering a sense of trust that can be crucial in negotiations.

One of the most notable examples of beer's role in diplomacy is its use during state visits and international summits. Leaders often partake in local brews to symbolize respect for the host country's culture and traditions. For instance, during a state visit to Germany, a U.S. president might be seen raising a glass of German lager, signaling a mutual appreciation and understanding between the two nations. Such gestures can serve to reinforce alliances and strengthen bilateral relations.

Beer also plays a significant role in trade agreements and economic diplomacy. Countries that produce renowned beer styles often use these products to promote their national identity and cultural heritage. For example, Belgium has leveraged its rich brewing tradition to engage in cultural diplomacy, showcasing its Trappist beers and lambics as symbols of craftsmanship and tradition. This not only enhances Belgium's cultural profile on the world stage but also opens doors for economic partnerships and trade discussions within the brewing industry.

Moreover, beer festivals and events frequently serve as informal venues for diplomatic engagement. International beer festivals, such as the Great American Beer Festival or Oktoberfest in Germany, attract brewers, industry professionals, and beer enthusiasts from around the world. These events provide an opportunity for networking and collaboration, where officials can engage in discussions about trade regulations, sustainability practices, and cultural exchange. By creating a convivial environment centered around beer, these festivals facilitate dialogue that might not occur in more formal settings.

In recent years, the rise of craft beer has added another layer to beer diplomacy. Many countries are experiencing a craft beer renaissance, with local brewers experimenting with diverse ingredients and brewing techniques. This innovation not only reflects cultural identity but also opens avenues for international collaboration. Countries with burgeoning craft beer scenes often look to partner with established brewing nations for knowledge exchange, fostering relationships that can extend beyond the brewing industry into broader diplomatic initiatives.

However, the use of beer in diplomacy is not without its challenges. Cultural sensitivities regarding alcohol consumption can complicate interactions, especially in predominantly Muslim countries where drinking is prohibited. In such contexts, diplomats must navigate these cultural norms carefully, often opting for non-alcoholic alternatives or engaging in discussions about beer in more abstract terms, focusing on brewing traditions rather than consumption.

In conclusion, beer's role in international relations is a testament to its power as a cultural artifact that transcends borders. Whether through shared toasts at state dinners, informal discussions at beer festivals, or as part of trade negotiations, beer has the potential to bridge cultural divides and foster diplomatic relationships. As the world continues to globalize, the importance of understanding and appreciating the cultural significance of beer in diplomacy will only grow, highlighting its unique ability to unite people across diverse backgrounds.

Chapter 10

The Rise of Craft Beer

The Craft Beer Revolution: Origins in the Late 20th Century

The late 20th century marked a significant turning point in the history of beer, heralding the rise of craft beer—a movement that transformed brewing from a large-scale industrial operation into a vibrant, community-driven craft. This revolution can be seen as a reaction against mass-produced beers that dominated the market, characterized by their uniformity and lack of distinct flavor. The origins of this movement are rooted in several socio-economic, cultural, and technological factors that converged in the 1970s and 1980s.

In the United States, the craft beer movement began taking shape in the wake of the 1970s, a period marked by a growing interest in artisanal products. As Americans became increasingly disenchanted with the homogenized offerings of major breweries—often referred to as "macrobrews"—a new wave of beer enthusiasts began to explore brewing as a hobby. The homebrewing movement gained traction following the legalization of homebrewing in 1978, as championed by President Jimmy Carter. This legislation allowed individuals to experiment with brewing techniques and diverse ingredients, leading to the creation of unique beer styles that were previously unavailable in the mainstream market.

By the early 1980s, the first wave of microbreweries began to emerge across the United States. Pioneering breweries such as Sierra Nevada Brewing Co., established in 1980, and Boston Beer Company, founded in 1984, were instrumental in popularizing craft beer. These breweries focused on quality ingredients, traditional brewing methods, and innovative flavors, laying the groundwork for what would become a thriving craft beer culture. Their success demonstrated that there was a considerable demand for diverse and flavorful beers, challenging the dominance of larger beer corporations.

The 1990s saw a dramatic surge in the number of craft breweries. The Brewers Association, founded in 2005, played a critical role in promoting and supporting the craft beer industry, providing resources and advocacy for small and independent brewers. By the end of the decade, the number of craft breweries in the United States had skyrocketed, from just over 100 in 1980 to nearly 1,500 by 1999. This expansion was fueled by a growing consumer interest in local and sustainable products, as well as a desire for authenticity in food and drink.
Moreover, the craft beer revolution was not just an American phenomenon; it had global implications. Countries such as the United Kingdom, Belgium, and Australia also experienced a

resurgence in small-scale, independent brewing during this period. In the UK, the Campaign for Real Ale (CAMRA), founded in 1971, advocated for traditional brewing methods and the preservation of cask ale, influencing the craft beer landscape in Europe. Meanwhile, Belgium's rich brewing heritage, characterized by a wide array of unique styles such as Trappist ales, lambics, and saisons, inspired many craft brewers to explore and innovate within these traditions.

The late 20th century also saw the emergence of beer festivals and competitions, which became vital platforms for showcasing craft beers and fostering a sense of community among brewers and consumers. Events like the Great American Beer Festival, launched in 1982, not only celebrated the diversity of craft beer but also provided a space for brewers to network and share ideas.

In conclusion, the craft beer revolution that originated in the late 20th century was a multifaceted movement driven by a collective desire for quality, diversity, and authenticity in beer. It reshaped the brewing landscape, empowering consumers to seek out unique flavors and local breweries, ultimately revitalizing a centuries-old tradition. This revolution laid the foundation for the modern craft beer industry we see today, characterized by an ever-expanding array of styles and a strong emphasis on local community engagement. The ripple effects of this movement continue to influence beer culture across the globe, proving that the craft beer revolution was not merely a trend but a lasting transformation in how we appreciate and enjoy beer.

Microbreweries and Brewpubs: A New Way of Brewing

The emergence of microbreweries and brewpubs represents a significant evolution in the brewing industry, reshaping not only how beer is produced but also how it is consumed and appreciated. The shift toward smaller-scale brewing operations began in the late 20th century and has since grown into a robust movement that champions craftsmanship, creativity, and local community engagement.

Microbreweries are defined as small, independent breweries that produce limited amounts of beer, typically characterized by their focus on quality, flavor, and traditional brewing methods. According to the Brewers Association, a microbrewery produces less than 15,000 barrels of beer annually, with a significant portion of its beer sold off-site. This contrasts sharply with large-scale commercial breweries that often prioritize mass production and consistency over unique flavor profiles.

The rise of microbreweries can be traced back to the craft beer movement, which gained momentum in the 1970s and 1980s as beer enthusiasts sought alternatives to mass-produced lagers and pilsners. The first wave of craft breweries emphasized traditional brewing techniques, using high-quality ingredients and innovative recipes to create distinctive flavors. This rebellion against the industrial beer landscape ignited a passion for craft brewing that continues to thrive today.

Brewpubs, on the other hand, are establishments that brew beer on-site and serve it alongside a menu of food. They provide a unique dining experience where patrons can enjoy a freshly brewed beer paired with thoughtfully prepared meals. Brewpubs not only facilitate the direct consumption of craft beer but also serve as community hubs, often reflecting local culture and fostering social interaction. Many brewpubs experiment with pairing their beers with food to enhance both the dining and drinking experience, showcasing the versatility of beer as a culinary companion.

One of the key factors contributing to the success of microbreweries and brewpubs is the emphasis on community and locality. These establishments often source ingredients from local farms, promoting sustainability and supporting regional economies. They create a sense of place, allowing consumers to connect with the source of their beverages while instilling a sense of pride in local products. This local-first approach resonates with consumers increasingly seeking authentic, hand-crafted experiences over mass-produced alternatives.

Microbreweries and brewpubs also foster innovation in brewing techniques and styles. Many brewers experiment with unconventional ingredients, such as fruits, spices, and herbs, pushing the boundaries of traditional beer styles. This spirit of experimentation has led to the creation of a wide variety of beer styles, including IPAs, stouts, sours, and barrel-aged brews, catering to diverse palates and preferences. Moreover, the collaborative nature of the craft beer community encourages brewers to share knowledge, techniques, and inspiration, further fueling creativity.

In addition to crafting unique beverages, microbreweries and brewpubs play a vital role in promoting beer culture through events, tastings, and festivals. They often host brewery tours, educational workshops, and beer-tasting events, allowing consumers to deepen their understanding of the brewing process and the nuances of different beer styles. This educational aspect fosters a more informed consumer base that appreciates the craftsmanship involved in brewing, leading to a more vibrant beer culture overall.

The rise of microbreweries and brewpubs has not only transformed the brewing landscape but has also influenced consumer behavior, encouraging a shift toward quality, locality, and community engagement in the beer industry. As these establishments continue to proliferate, they will undoubtedly play a crucial role in shaping the future of beer, celebrating innovation while honoring traditional brewing practices. The craft beer movement, embodied by microbreweries and brewpubs, champions a deeper connection between the brewer and the consumer, ensuring that the appreciation for beer as a cultural and culinary staple remains strong in modern society.

The Role of Craft Beer in Local Economies

Craft beer has emerged as more than just a refreshing beverage; it plays a significant role in local economies, influencing job creation, tourism, community development, and local agriculture. The craft beer movement, which gained momentum in the late 20th century, has transformed the brewing landscape, fostering a culture of innovation and entrepreneurship that benefits communities across the globe.

Job Creation and Economic Impact

One of the most immediate impacts of the craft beer industry on local economies is job creation. Craft breweries, often small and independently owned, require a diverse workforce that includes brewers, marketing professionals, sales staff, and hospitality workers. According to the Brewers Association, the craft brewing industry supports hundreds of thousands of jobs in the United States alone, with many craft breweries employing a handful to several dozen people directly. Moreover, these breweries generate additional employment opportunities in related sectors, such as distribution, retail, and agriculture, contributing to a robust employment ecosystem.

In addition to direct employment, craft breweries stimulate local economies through their supply chains. They often partner with local farmers for ingredients like hops and barley, fostering agricultural jobs and promoting sustainable farming practices. This local sourcing not only reduces transportation costs and carbon footprints but also strengthens community ties, as both brewers and farmers become invested in each other's success.

Tourism and Community Engagement

Craft breweries have also become major attractions for tourists. Brewery tours, tastings, and festivals draw visitors from outside the area, generating revenue for local businesses, including restaurants, hotels, and shops. Events like beer festivals often showcase both local and regional breweries, creating a vibrant atmosphere that celebrates community and craft. This influx of tourists not only benefits the breweries but also enhances the overall visibility and appeal of the locality as a destination.

Moreover, craft beer fosters community engagement. Many breweries serve as social hubs, providing spaces for locals to gather, share stories, and build relationships. Taprooms and brewpubs often host events such as trivia nights, live music, and charity fundraisers, which further enrich community life and encourage social interaction. This sense of belonging and community pride can lead to increased local spending, as residents are more likely to support businesses that contribute positively to their neighborhoods.

Supporting Local Agriculture
The craft beer movement has revived interest in local agriculture, particularly in the cultivation of ingredients traditionally used in brewing. Many craft brewers prioritize sourcing local hops, barley, and even specialty ingredients like fruits and spices. This not only supports local farmers but also promotes biodiversity and sustainable farming practices. As craft breweries advocate for local sourcing, they encourage consumers to appreciate the unique flavors and characteristics of regional ingredients, thus creating a stronger connection between the brewery and its community.

Challenges and Opportunities
Despite its many benefits, the craft beer industry faces challenges that can impact local economies. Competition from large multinational breweries and increasing regulatory pressures can threaten the viability of small craft operations. However, the industry's resilience and adaptability have led to innovative approaches, such as the rise of brewpubs and the use of social media for marketing and community engagement.

In conclusion, the role of craft beer in local economies is multifaceted and significant. Through job creation, tourism, community engagement, and support for local agriculture, craft breweries contribute to the economic vitality of their regions. As consumers increasingly seek authentic, local experiences, the craft beer movement is poised to continue its expansion, further embedding itself in the social and economic fabric of communities worldwide. The future of craft beer not only promises diverse flavors and innovative brewing techniques but also a continued commitment to cultivating local economies and fostering community connections.

Beer Styles in the Craft Movement: IPAs, Stouts, and Sours
The craft beer movement, which gained significant traction in the late 20th century, has not only revolutionized how beer is produced and consumed but also diversified the range of beer styles available to enthusiasts. Among these, India Pale Ales (IPAs), stouts, and sours stand out as essential representations of this renaissance in brewing, each embodying unique characteristics, histories, and cultural significance.

India Pale Ales (IPAs)
IPAs have become synonymous with the craft beer movement, celebrated for their bold hop flavors and higher alcohol content. Originating in England in the 19th century, IPAs were initially brewed with extra hops to preserve the beer during long sea voyages to India. This preservation method inadvertently led to the development of a distinctively bitter and aromatic beer style that became popular among British colonizers.

The modern craft scene has taken IPAs to new heights, with substyles like West Coast, New England (or Hazy), and Double IPAs. West Coast IPAs are characterized by their clear appearance and a pronounced bitterness balanced with citrus and pine notes, often resulting from the use of American hop varieties. In contrast, New England IPAs boast a hazy appearance and a juicy, tropical fruit-forward profile, achieved through late hopping techniques and the use of specific yeast strains that contribute to their smooth mouthfeel. Double IPAs amplify these characteristics, offering higher alcohol content and intense hop flavors, appealing to those who crave bold and robust brews.

The craft beer revolution has also inspired experimentation within the IPA category, leading to innovative approaches like the use of unconventional hops, adjuncts, and even blending with other beer styles. The result is an ever-evolving landscape of IPAs that captivates drinkers and challenges traditional notions of beer.

Stouts

Stouts, with their rich, dark appearance and complex flavors, are another cornerstone of the craft beer movement. This style traces its roots back to the 18th century in England, where it evolved from porters—a dark beer brewed with roasted malt. Stouts typically feature flavors of coffee, chocolate, and caramel, with varying levels of sweetness and bitterness depending on the brewing process.

The most famous stout is arguably the Irish Dry Stout, exemplified by Guinness, known for its creamy head and roasted malt flavors. However, craft brewers have expanded the stout category significantly, introducing variations such as Milk Stouts, which incorporate lactose for sweetness, and Imperial Stouts, which boast higher alcohol content and a more intense flavor profile.

Additionally, the craft movement has seen the emergence of barrel-aged stouts, where the beer is aged in whiskey or bourbon barrels, imparting unique flavors and complexity. These innovations have broadened the appeal of stouts beyond traditional drinkers, attracting a new generation of enthusiasts eager to explore the depths of this rich and flavorful style.

Sours

Sour beers represent a fascinating and complex segment of the craft movement, characterized by their tartness and unique fermentation processes. The resurgence of sour beers can be attributed to a growing interest in traditional brewing methods and the exploration of wild yeast strains and bacteria, such as Brettanomyces and Lactobacillus, which contribute to their distinctive sour flavors.

Belgian-style sours, like Lambics and Flanders Reds, have inspired many craft brewers. These beers often undergo spontaneous fermentation, allowing wild yeast and bacteria from the environment to influence their flavor profiles. American craft brewers have embraced this style, creating their own interpretations, such as Berliner Weisse and Gose, which are known for their refreshing tartness and are often enhanced with fruit for added complexity.

The craft beer movement has played a pivotal role in demystifying sour beers, encouraging experimentation and innovation. Many breweries now offer sour programs that showcase the art of blending and aging, leading to a diverse range of sour offerings that appeal to adventurous palates.

In conclusion, IPAs, stouts, and sours are not just beer styles; they are reflections of the creativity and passion that define the craft beer movement. As brewers continue to experiment and push boundaries, these styles will undoubtedly evolve, offering new experiences and flavors for beer lovers around the world.

Craft Beer Festivals and Tasting Events

The craft beer movement, which began in earnest in the late 20th century, has fostered a vibrant culture of beer appreciation that culminates in the popularity of craft beer festivals and tasting events. These gatherings serve as a confluence for brewers, enthusiasts, and the curious, celebrating not only the diversity of flavors and brewing techniques but also the community spirit that craft beer embodies.

A Celebration of Diversity

Craft beer festivals are characterized by their vast selection of unique brews, often highlighting local microbreweries and independent brands. Unlike larger, mass-produced beers, craft beers are known for their innovation and creativity, with brewers experimenting with ingredients, styles, and brewing methods. Festivals typically feature a range of beer styles—from IPAs and stouts to sours and barrel-aged creations—allowing attendees to explore a spectrum of flavors and aromas. This diversity is a reflection of the brewers' commitment to quality and craftsmanship, as well as their desire to push the boundaries of traditional brewing.

Building Community Connections

At their core, craft beer festivals foster community. They bring together brewers, patrons, and local businesses, creating an environment that encourages interaction and exchange. Attendees often have the opportunity to meet the brewers behind their favorite beers, learning about the inspiration and processes that go into each brew. This personal connection enhances the drinking experience, transforming casual consumers into passionate advocates for specific brands and styles.

Furthermore, many craft beer festivals also emphasize local foods, featuring food trucks and local restaurants that pair their offerings with the featured beers. This synergistic relationship not only promotes local cuisine but also enhances the overall experience, as attendees can enjoy complementary flavors that elevate both the food and the beer.

Education and Engagement

Craft beer festivals also serve an educational purpose, offering seminars, tastings, and workshops led by industry experts. These sessions can cover a range of topics, such as brewing techniques, food pairings, and the science of fermentation. By providing attendees with insights into the brewing process and the nuances of flavor profiles, festivals cultivate a more informed drinking culture. This educational aspect is crucial in demystifying craft beer, making it more accessible to newcomers who might feel intimidated by the wide array of choices.

The Evolution of Craft Beer Events

Over the years, craft beer festivals have evolved from small gatherings into large-scale events that attract thousands of participants. Iconic festivals like the Great American Beer Festival in Denver and the Oregon Brewers Festival in Portland have become must-attend occasions for beer lovers. These events not only feature tastings but also competitions where breweries showcase their best brews, often leading to prestigious awards that can significantly elevate a brewery's reputation.

In addition to traditional festivals, tasting events have also gained popularity. These more intimate gatherings focus on specific themes, such as seasonal brews, regional specialties, or innovative brewing techniques. Tasting events often provide a curated experience, allowing participants to delve deeper into specific styles or trends within the craft beer landscape.

Impact on the Craft Beer Industry

The rise of craft beer festivals and tasting events has had a profound impact on the craft beer industry as a whole. They serve as crucial marketing platforms for breweries, enabling them to reach new customers and build brand loyalty. As attendees discover new favorites, they often seek out these beers in their local markets, thereby driving sales and expanding the reach of craft breweries.

Moreover, these events contribute to the local economy, generating revenue not only for breweries but also for associated businesses such as hotels, restaurants, and transportation services. By creating a vibrant ecosystem surrounding craft beer, festivals play a significant role in the growth and sustainability of the industry.

In conclusion, craft beer festivals and tasting events are more than just opportunities to sample unique brews; they are celebrations of community, education, and innovation within the craft beer movement. As they continue to grow in popularity, these gatherings will undoubtedly remain central to the craft beer experience, fostering a culture of appreciation and camaraderie among beer enthusiasts and brewers alike.

Chapter 11

Beer and Health

The Historical Belief in Beer as Medicine

Throughout history, beer has occupied a unique place not only as a social drink but also as a substance believed to possess medicinal properties. This perception of beer as a therapeutic beverage spans various cultures and epochs, revealing the complex interplay between health, nutrition, and social practices.

The earliest record of beer being used for medicinal purposes can be traced back to the ancient civilizations of Mesopotamia and Egypt. The Sumerians, who are among the first to document brewing practices, recognized beer not merely as a recreational drink but as a source of nourishment and health. They brewed beer using barley, which was believed to provide energy and vital nutrients. Tablets from this era depict beer as an essential dietary component, often consumed by workers, particularly those engaged in strenuous labor such as building ziggurats or agriculture.

In ancient Egypt, beer was a staple in the daily diet and was consumed by all social classes, from pharaohs to laborers. The Egyptians attributed various healing properties to beer, often used in rituals and as a remedy for ailments. For instance, beer was used to treat digestive issues and was even prescribed for childbirth, underlining its perceived role as a tonic for both physical and reproductive health. Ancient Egyptian texts document that beer was often mixed with medicinal herbs to enhance its therapeutic effects, highlighting an early understanding of the relationship between substances and health.

As we move into the classical period, the Greeks and Romans also embraced the medicinal qualities of beer. Hippocrates, often referred to as the "Father of Medicine," acknowledged beer's health benefits, recommending it for various ailments, including fevers and digestive disorders. Roman soldiers consumed beer to maintain their strength and health, with certain varieties believed to bolster the immune system. This practice further propagated the idea that beer was not merely a pleasurable indulgence but a necessary dietary element that could promote health and wellness.

During the Middle Ages in Europe, beer continued to be viewed as a medicinal beverage. Monasteries played a crucial role in brewing, and monks often produced beer not only for sustenance but also for its perceived health benefits. It was common for monks to brew specific types of beer infused with herbs and spices, believed to treat various ailments. The brewing process was viewed as an alchemical art, where fermentation was thought to enhance the drink's healing properties.

The association of beer with health persisted into the Renaissance and Enlightenment periods when it became increasingly recognized for its nutritional value. Scholars began to study the composition of beer, understanding that its fermentation process produced essential vitamins and minerals. Physicians began prescribing beer for its caloric content, especially for patients recovering from illness or those unable to consume solid food.

In the 19th century, the rise of modern medicine began to challenge traditional beliefs about beer as a health tonic. However, even then, it was not uncommon for doctors to recommend moderate beer consumption for its supposed health benefits. Beer was often marketed as a restorative beverage, especially for convalescents and the elderly.

Today, while the medical community has shifted focus to more scientifically validated treatments, the historical belief in beer as a form of medicine remains a fascinating aspect of its cultural legacy. Contemporary studies have explored potential health benefits associated with moderate beer consumption, including cardiovascular health and social well-being. Although the medical claims of ancient times may not hold up to modern scrutiny, they illustrate the longstanding human relationship with beer as more than a mere recreational drink—one that has intertwined with our notions of health and wellness throughout history.

The Nutritional Value of Beer: Myths and Facts

Beer has been a staple in many cultures for thousands of years, often celebrated for its social and cultural significance. However, the nutritional value of beer is frequently misunderstood, leading to various myths and misconceptions. This section aims to clarify the facts surrounding beer's nutritional profile, its health implications, and its place in a balanced diet.

Nutritional Composition

Beer is primarily composed of water, which can constitute up to 90-95% of its content. The remaining components include carbohydrates, proteins, and small amounts of fat. The specific nutritional values can vary based on the type of beer, the brewing process, and the ingredients used. **Typically, a standard 12-ounce (355 ml) serving of beer contains approximately:**

- **Calories:** Between 150 to 200 calories, depending on the style. Light beers may have around 100 calories, while stronger ales and stouts can exceed 300.
- **Carbohydrates:** Roughly 10-15 grams, which primarily come from residual sugars left after fermentation.
- **Proteins:** Approximately 1-2 grams, with the primary source being the malt used in brewing.
- **Vitamins and Minerals:** Beer contains small amounts of vitamins B6, B12, niacin, riboflavin, and folate, as well as minerals such as potassium, magnesium, and phosphorus.

Myths Surrounding Beer

1. Beer is a Good Source of Nutrients: While beer does contain certain vitamins and minerals, it is not a substitute for a balanced diet. The amounts are relatively low compared to other food sources, and excessive consumption can lead to negative health effects.

2. Beer Makes You Fat: The notion that beer is solely responsible for weight gain is an oversimplification. Weight gain occurs when there is a caloric surplus, regardless of the source. While beer does contribute calories, it can be consumed in moderation as part of a balanced diet without leading to weight gain.

3. Beer is Hydrating: Many believe that beer can hydrate the body. However, due to its alcohol content, beer is actually a diuretic, causing increased urination and potential dehydration. It is essential to drink water alongside alcoholic beverages to maintain proper hydration.

Health Benefits of Beer

When consumed in moderation, beer may offer some health benefits. Studies have indicated that moderate beer consumption can be linked to several positive health outcomes:

1. Cardiovascular Health: Moderate beer drinkers have been shown to have a lower risk of heart disease compared to heavy drinkers or non-drinkers. This is often attributed to the presence of antioxidants in beer, such as polyphenols, which can help reduce inflammation and improve heart health.

2. Bone Health: Research suggests that the silicon present in beer, particularly in pale ales, may contribute to bone density and strength, potentially reducing the risk of osteoporosis.

3. Social Benefits: The role of beer as a social lubricant cannot be understated. Moderate consumption in social settings can enhance social interactions, reduce stress, and improve overall well-being.

Responsible Drinking
While beer does have some nutritional value and potential health benefits, it is crucial to consume it responsibly. The key is moderation. Most health guidelines suggest that moderate drinking is defined as up to one drink per day for women and up to two drinks per day for men. Excessive drinking can lead to numerous health problems, including liver disease, addiction, and increased risk of certain cancers.

Conclusion
Understanding the nutritional value of beer involves separating myths from facts. While it can contribute certain nutrients and offer potential health benefits, it should not be viewed as a health food. As with any alcoholic beverage, moderation is essential for enjoying beer as part of a healthy lifestyle. The enjoyment of beer should always be balanced with an awareness of its effects and a commitment to responsible consumption.

The Impact of Beer on Public Health
The relationship between beer consumption and public health is a multifaceted topic that intertwines cultural, social, and physiological dimensions. Historically, beer has been both lauded for its potential health benefits and scrutinized for its adverse effects. Understanding this duality requires a careful examination of the nutritional value of beer, its historical context as a medicinal substance, and the implications of its consumption patterns in modern society.

Historical Perspective on Beer as Medicine
Beer has a long-standing reputation as a medicinal beverage. In ancient civilizations, it was often prescribed for a variety of ailments. In Mesopotamia, for instance, beer was considered a safer alternative to water, which was frequently contaminated. As a result, it became a staple in daily diets, providing hydration and calories. The Sumerians and Egyptians noted its nutritional benefits, and it was commonly used in ceremonial contexts as well as in therapeutic practices. Ancient texts highlight the use of beer in treating ailments like digestive issues and as a source of energy for laborers.

Nutritional Value of Beer
Beer contains several nutrients that can contribute to health when consumed in moderation. It is made primarily from water, barley, hops, and yeast, and is rich in vitamins such as B vitamins (including B6, niacin, and riboflavin) and minerals like magnesium and potassium. The presence of antioxidants, particularly polyphenols, has been linked to various health benefits, including the potential to reduce inflammation and combat oxidative stress.

However, it is crucial to recognize that these benefits are most pronounced in moderate consumption. The definition of moderation varies, but many health organizations suggest that this equates to up to one drink per day for women and up to two for men. Excessive consumption, on the other hand, can lead to a range of health issues, including liver disease, cardiovascular problems, and addiction.

Public Health Concerns and Alcohol Abuse

The darker side of beer consumption is its potential to contribute to public health crises, particularly in the context of alcohol abuse. The World Health Organization (WHO) reports significant health risks associated with excessive drinking, which is linked to accidents, injuries, and chronic diseases. In the United States, for example, the National Institute on Alcohol Abuse and Alcoholism (NIAAA) highlights that alcohol misuse is a major public health concern, leading to increased healthcare costs and societal burdens.

The impact of beer on public health is particularly evident in discussions surrounding binge drinking and alcohol dependency. These issues are exacerbated in certain demographics, such as young adults and college students, where social norms may promote excessive drinking. Public health campaigns often focus on the need for responsible drinking and awareness of the risks associated with high alcohol consumption.

The Role of Responsible Drinking

In response to the health risks associated with beer, many organizations advocate for responsible drinking practices. Education plays a key role in this approach, emphasizing moderation and awareness of personal limits. Communities are increasingly focused on fostering environments that support healthy drinking habits, such as promoting non-alcoholic options and encouraging social activities that do not center around alcohol consumption.

Moreover, the craft beer movement has also shifted the narrative around beer consumption. Many craft breweries promote responsible drinking and sustainability, often partnering with local organizations to raise awareness about the importance of moderation and the impact of alcohol on health. This cultural shift towards appreciating beer for its craftsmanship rather than solely for its intoxicating effects can positively influence public health perceptions.

Conclusion

The impact of beer on public health is a complex interplay of benefits and risks. While moderate consumption can offer certain health advantages, excessive drinking poses significant health threats. Public health initiatives aimed at promoting responsible drinking and education about alcohol's effects are crucial in mitigating risks. As beer continues to evolve in the context of modern society, fostering a balanced perspective on its consumption will be essential for promoting healthy lifestyles.

Beer and the "Beer Belly": Separating Fact from Fiction

The term "beer belly" refers colloquially to the abdominal weight gain that some associate with beer consumption. This phrase is often used to caricature the appearance of individuals who drink large quantities of beer, suggesting a direct correlation between beer intake and the accumulation of abdominal fat. However, to understand the nuances of this concept, it is essential to delve into the science of nutrition, metabolism, and lifestyle factors.

Understanding Body Fat Accumulation

Body fat accumulation is a complex process influenced by numerous factors, including total caloric intake, physical activity levels, genetic predisposition, and overall dietary patterns. While beer does contain calories—approximately 150 calories per 12-ounce serving of regular beer—it's crucial to recognize that the consumption of any high-calorie beverage can lead to weight gain if it contributes to a caloric surplus. Hence, the blame cannot rest solely on beer; rather, it is the total caloric intake from all food and beverages that matters most.

The Role of Beer in Diet

Beer, like other alcoholic beverages, contributes calories to one's diet but lacks significant nutritional value. It is primarily composed of water, carbohydrates, and alcohol, with minimal vitamins and minerals. When consumed in moderation, beer can fit into a balanced diet. However, excessive consumption, particularly in conjunction with a diet high in sugars and fats, can lead to weight gain and the development of a "beer belly."

Alcohol Metabolism

Alcohol is metabolized differently from food. The body prioritizes the metabolism of alcohol over other macronutrients. When alcohol is consumed, it is broken down in the liver, and this process can temporarily halt the oxidation of fats and carbohydrates. This means that when one consumes beer, especially in large quantities, the body's ability to burn fat is diminished, potentially leading to fat storage, particularly around the abdomen.

Lifestyle Factors

The lifestyle associated with beer consumption often plays a significant role in the development of a beer belly. Drinking beer is frequently accompanied by social gatherings and sedentary activities, such as watching sports or attending parties, which can lead to decreased physical activity. Additionally, beer is often consumed alongside calorie-dense snacks, further exacerbating the caloric intake problem.

The Myth of the Beer Belly
The stereotype of the beer belly has become ingrained in popular culture, leading to the misconception that beer is the sole culprit behind abdominal weight gain. In reality, the relationship between beer consumption and weight gain is influenced by broader dietary habits and lifestyle choices. Individuals who consume beer but maintain a balanced diet and engage in regular exercise may not experience any significant weight gain.

Moderation and Mindful Consumption
For those concerned about the potential impact of beer on body composition, moderation is key. Drinking beer in reasonable quantities, choosing lower-calorie options, and complementing beer consumption with a balanced diet and regular physical activity can help mitigate the risk of weight gain. Furthermore, being mindful of portion sizes and the frequency of consumption can contribute to maintaining a healthy weight.

Conclusion
In summary, while the notion of a "beer belly" captures public imagination, it oversimplifies a complex issue involving caloric intake, metabolism, and lifestyle. Beer itself is not inherently responsible for abdominal weight gain; rather, it is the context in which it is consumed that matters. By adopting a balanced approach to diet and lifestyle, individuals can enjoy beer as part of a healthy lifestyle without succumbing to the stereotype of the beer belly.

Responsible Drinking: Moderation and Enjoyment
Beer, one of the oldest and most widely consumed beverages in the world, has long been associated with social gatherings, celebrations, and cultural traditions. However, with its popularity comes the responsibility of understanding and promoting responsible drinking practices. This section delves into the importance of moderation and enjoyment, highlighting the balance necessary for a healthier relationship with alcohol.

Understanding Moderation
Moderation in drinking is often defined by the quantity consumed and the frequency of consumption. National health organizations, such as the Centers for Disease Control and Prevention (CDC) and the National Institute on Alcohol Abuse and Alcoholism (NIAAA), provide guidelines for what constitutes moderate drinking. Generally, this is defined as up to one drink per day for women and up to two drinks per day for men. A standard drink is typically defined as 14 grams of pure alcohol, which is roughly equivalent to a 12-ounce beer with about 5% alcohol by volume (ABV).

Understanding moderation is crucial not only for individual health but also for fostering a social environment that encourages responsible consumption. Drinking in moderation can minimize risks associated with alcohol, including impaired judgment, addiction, and long-term health issues such as liver disease and cardiovascular problems.

The Importance of Enjoyment

Moderate drinking is not just about limiting intake; it is also about enhancing the enjoyment of beer as a beverage. The experience of drinking beer can be enriched by savoring its flavors, appreciating its craftsmanship, and understanding its cultural significance. This enjoyment can be heightened through activities such as beer tasting, food pairings, and attending local breweries or beer festivals.

When individuals focus on the quality of their drinking experience rather than the quantity, they often find that they can still partake socially without overindulgence. For instance, savoring a well-crafted IPA or a rich stout can be a more fulfilling experience than consuming beer mindlessly. Engaging with the beer community—joining tastings, participating in brewery tours, or learning about brewing processes—can cultivate a deeper appreciation for the beverage that promotes responsible drinking practices.

The Role of Social Settings

Social settings play a significant role in drinking behaviors. Beer is often consumed during gatherings such as barbecues, celebrations, and sporting events. In these environments, peer pressure and the desire to fit in can sometimes lead to excessive drinking. Education about responsible drinking can help mitigate these pressures. Encouraging conversations about moderation, offering non-alcoholic alternatives, and promoting designated drivers can foster a culture where enjoyment and safety go hand in hand.

Moreover, public awareness campaigns aimed at promoting responsible drinking can help shift societal norms. Initiatives that celebrate moderation—such as "Mindful Drinking Month" or "Sober October"—encourage individuals to reflect on their drinking habits and consider their health and well-being.

Conclusion

In conclusion, responsible drinking encompasses both moderation and enjoyment. By adhering to guidelines for moderate consumption, individuals can appreciate beer's rich history and diverse flavors while minimizing health risks. Enjoyment of beer should be celebrated as a cultural and social experience, one that fosters connections and enhances life's moments. As society continues to evolve in its understanding of alcohol consumption, promoting responsible drinking will be vital in ensuring that beer remains a source of joy and community, rather than a cause for concern. Through education, awareness, and a focus on quality over quantity, beer can be enjoyed responsibly for generations to come.

Chapter 12

Beer and Art

Beer in Literature: From Ancient Poems to Modern Novels

Beer has been an integral part of human culture for millennia, serving as both a social lubricant and a source of inspiration for writers across generations. Its presence in literature is as diverse as the beverage itself, reflecting societal values, rituals, and personal experiences. From ancient texts to contemporary novels, beer has been a symbol of camaraderie, festivity, and even rebellion, weaving its way into the fabric of storytelling.

Ancient Texts and Epic Poetry

The earliest references to beer in literature can be traced back to ancient civilizations, particularly in Mesopotamia where the Sumerians revered it. The "Hymn to Ninkasi," a 1800 BCE poem, not only celebrates the goddess of beer but also serves as one of the oldest known recipes for brewing. This text underscores the importance of beer in daily life and religious ceremonies, illustrating how it was intertwined with both the mundane and the divine.

Similarly, the "Epic of Gilgamesh," one of the oldest known works of literature, features beer prominently. The character Enkidu, created by the gods, is transformed from a wild man into a civilized being after consuming beer, highlighting its role as a catalyst for socialization and cultural development. Such early works illustrate how beer transcended mere consumption; it was a vehicle for storytelling, reflecting the values and belief systems of the time.

Classical Literature and Social Commentary

As literature evolved through classical antiquity, references to beer continued to appear. In ancient Greece, playwrights like Aristophanes incorporated beer into their comedies, often using it as a device to explore themes of excess, revelry, and the human condition. The drink was a staple at symposia, gatherings that celebrated intellectual discourse accompanied by wine and beer, emphasizing its role in social interaction and community bonding.

In Roman literature, beer was often depicted with a sense of disdain compared to wine, but it still found its way into works by authors like Pliny the Elder, who acknowledged the brewing practices of various cultures. This duality in perception reflects wider societal attitudes toward different alcoholic beverages, providing a lens through which we can examine cultural biases and preferences.

Medieval and Renaissance Literature
The Middle Ages saw beer's significance continue in the literary world, especially in the context of the monastery. Monks, who were some of the most skilled brewers of the time, often wrote about their brewing practices in religious texts. These narratives not only documented the brewing process but also the spiritual significance of beer, linking it to notions of hospitality and charity.

The Renaissance brought a renewed focus on humanism and creativity, where beer appeared in the works of Shakespeare, who used it to illustrate character traits and social class. In plays like "Henry IV," the tavern setting serves as a backdrop for themes of friendship, loyalty, and conflict, with beer acting as a unifying element among the characters.

Modern Novels and Cultural Reflection
In contemporary literature, beer remains a prevalent motif, often symbolizing community, identity, and cultural heritage. Authors like Charles Bukowski and John Steinbeck have depicted beer as a reflection of the human experience—its highs and lows. Bukowski's semi-autobiographical works frequently highlight the role of beer in the lives of the marginalized, while Steinbeck often depicted it as a form of solace during difficult times.

Moreover, modern novels have seen the rise of craft beer culture, exploring themes of authenticity and artisanal production in a world dominated by mass consumption. Books like "The Beer Book" and "The Art of Beer" delve into the craft brewing movement, celebrating the resurgence of local breweries and the stories behind their creations.

Conclusion
From ancient hymns to modern novels, beer has not only been a beverage but also a powerful narrative device. Its role in literature reflects broader societal trends, capturing the essence of human experience—celebration, struggle, and community. As long as beer continues to be brewed, it will undoubtedly remain a rich subject for writers, inspiring stories that resonate with readers across the globe.

The Role of Beer in Visual Art
Beer, one of humanity's oldest beverages, has inspired countless expressions of creativity in the realm of visual art. From ancient depictions in murals and pottery to contemporary advertisements and branding, beer has served as both a subject and a muse for artists across

cultures and eras. Its presence in visual art not only reflects the cultural significance of beer but also showcases its role as an essential element of social life.

Historical Depictions
The relationship between beer and art can be traced back to the earliest civilizations. In ancient Mesopotamia, for instance, beer was a staple of daily life and featured prominently in the art of the time. Sumerian tablets often depicted scenes of brewing and drinking, illustrating the importance of beer in religious rituals and social gatherings. Similarly, in ancient Egypt, tomb paintings frequently portrayed banquets where beer was consumed, signifying its role in both the afterlife and daily existence.

During the Renaissance, beer continued to gain prominence in art. Artists like Pieter Bruegel the Elder captured the essence of peasant life, often depicting communal feasts with beer as a central theme. Such paintings not only showcased the beverage but also served as social commentary on the lives of ordinary people, their joys, and their struggles.

Advertisements and Brand Identity
With the advent of mass production and the rise of the brewing industry in the 19th century, beer advertising became a significant aspect of visual culture. Breweries began to utilize art as a means to create memorable brand identities. Iconic advertisements featured vivid imagery and clever slogans that appealed to consumers' emotions and aspirations.

One of the most notable examples is the artwork of the famous beer poster artist, Edward Penfield, who captured the essence of turn-of-the-century America through his vibrant and stylized designs. His posters often depicted leisurely scenes of people enjoying beer, evoking a sense of camaraderie and celebration. Such advertisements not only promoted specific brands but also reinforced the cultural significance of beer as a social lubricant.

In the 20th century, the use of graphic design in beer advertising evolved dramatically. Breweries began to adopt modernist aesthetics, employing bold colors and clean lines to create striking visual identities. Brands like Heineken and Guinness developed distinct logos and packaging that became instantly recognizable, cementing their place in popular culture. The visual language of beer branding has continued to evolve, with contemporary craft breweries often embracing unique and artistic labels that reflect their brewing philosophy.

Beer in Contemporary Art
Today, beer remains a relevant subject in contemporary art. Artists often explore themes of consumption, identity, and community through the lens of beer culture. Installations,

sculptures, and mixed media works frequently incorporate beer-related imagery, challenging societal norms and perceptions surrounding alcohol consumption. Additionally, beer festivals and events often feature art displays that celebrate this beloved beverage, blurring the lines between culinary and visual art.

Moreover, beer has become a topic of exploration in advertising as brands seek to connect with younger audiences. Social media campaigns harness the power of visual storytelling, utilizing eye-catching graphics and engaging content to promote their products. This modern approach to branding not only highlights the beverage itself but also creates a narrative around the experiences associated with beer drinking—friendship, celebration, and enjoyment.

Conclusion
The role of beer in visual art is multifaceted, reflecting its significance throughout history as a symbol of culture, community, and social interaction. From ancient murals to modern advertisements, beer has inspired artists to explore its many dimensions, making it a vital part of our cultural heritage. As beer continues to evolve in both taste and presentation, so too will its representation in the world of visual art, ensuring that this storied beverage remains at the forefront of creative expression.

Beer in Music: Songs, Ballads, and Pub Culture
Beer has long been intertwined with music and cultural expression, serving as both inspiration and a backdrop for a multitude of songs, ballads, and communal gatherings. The relationship between beer and music is as old as the beverage itself, with historical roots that can be traced back to ancient societies where both were integral to social life. The communal act of drinking beer often transformed into communal singing, creating a vibrant tapestry of sounds that enhanced the drinking experience.

Historical Context
In many cultures, beer was consumed in public houses, taverns, and inns, where patrons would gather not just to drink but to engage in social activities, including singing. The earliest evidence of beer consumption in Mesopotamia and Egypt aligns with the rise of communal gatherings, where music played a crucial role in enhancing the atmosphere. Ancient Sumerians, for instance, celebrated their deities with hymns sung during festivals that also involved beer offerings, highlighting how these elements were interwoven in religious and social practices.

Traditional Beer Songs
Throughout history, various cultures have cultivated a rich tradition of beer songs that serve different purposes—from celebrating good times to lamenting lost love. In the British Isles, for

example, the tradition of the pub song emerged prominently. Songs like "Danny Boy" and "Wild Rover" became staples in pubs, allowing patrons to join in harmony, creating a sense of camaraderie among drinkers. These songs often tell stories of life, love, and loss, resonating with the emotions experienced during shared moments over pints of beer.

In Germany, the beer hall culture has given rise to a plethora of "Schunkellieder," or sing-along songs, that are sung during Oktoberfest and other beer festivals. These songs often have catchy refrains that encourage participation, reinforcing the social bonds among attendees and making the experience of enjoying a lager or wheat beer even more memorable.

The Role of Pub Culture
Pubs and taverns have been the backbone of musical expression surrounding beer. These establishments have historically served as venues for local musicians to perform folk songs, ballads, and traditional music. The informal nature of pubs allows for a spontaneous exchange of music, where patrons may even join in, turning a simple drinking session into a lively concert. This participatory culture has helped preserve folk traditions, passing them down through generations.

Moreover, the rise of folk festivals and beer fests has further enriched this connection. Many festivals celebrate both beer and music, offering a platform for local and international artists to perform. Events like the Great American Beer Festival feature live music alongside tastings, showcasing how beer can elevate the cultural experience.

Contemporary Trends
In modern society, the relationship between beer and music continues to thrive, albeit in new forms. The craft beer movement has inspired a wave of breweries that incorporate music into their branding and events. Many craft brewers host live music nights, encouraging local bands to perform while patrons enjoy unique brews. This not only enhances the tasting experience but also fosters community engagement and support for local artists.

Additionally, popular songs about beer have permeated mainstream music, with artists across genres celebrating the drink. Tracks like Toby Keith's "Beer for My Horses" and Jimmy Buffett's "Beer in Mexico" solidify beer's place in the lyrical canon, reflecting the lifestyle and values associated with beer culture.

Conclusion
The intersection of beer and music is a testament to humanity's enduring love for communal experiences. From the sung verses of ancient cultures to contemporary pub performances, beer

has played a significant role in shaping musical traditions around the world. As we continue to celebrate both beer and music, we uphold a rich cultural legacy that connects us through rhythm, melody, and, of course, good company over a shared drink.

The Aesthetic of Beer: Labels, Logos, and Packaging

In the world of brewing, beer transcends beyond mere liquid; it embodies a culture, a history, and an identity. The aesthetics of beer—specifically its labels, logos, and packaging—play a critical role in shaping consumer perceptions, influencing purchase decisions, and conveying the essence of the brewery's brand. As the craft beer movement has surged in popularity, the visual representation of beer has become increasingly sophisticated, innovative, and integral to the brewing experience.

The Importance of Labels

The label on a beer bottle or can serves as both a canvas and a storyteller. It is often the first point of contact between the consumer and the product, making it paramount for breweries to create visually striking designs that capture attention. A well-designed label communicates essential information, such as the beer style, the ingredients, the brewery's name, and sometimes even the story behind the brew.

For microbreweries and craft brewers, labels often reflect the unique character of the beer, incorporating local themes, whimsical illustrations, or historical references. Many breweries embrace hand-drawn art or vintage designs to evoke a sense of authenticity and craftsmanship. For instance, the use of bold colors and playful graphics can suggest an adventurous, hoppy IPA, while earthy tones and minimalist designs might indicate a more traditional lager or farmhouse ale.

Logos: Branding and Recognition

The logo is another vital element of a beer's aesthetic, encapsulating the brewery's identity and values. A well-crafted logo should be memorable, easily recognizable, and convey the brand's personality. For instance, the logo of a brewery that emphasizes sustainability may incorporate natural imagery, while one that focuses on innovation might feature modern, sleek typography.

As competition in the beer market intensifies, having a distinctive logo has never been more critical. A strong logo can foster brand loyalty, as consumers often gravitate toward familiar symbols, especially in crowded retail spaces or at bars. For example, iconic logos like the green bottle of Heineken or the red star of Budweiser are instantly recognizable across the globe.

Packaging Innovations

Packaging is an essential aspect of the beer aesthetic that extends beyond labels and logos. As consumer preferences shift towards sustainability, breweries are adopting eco-friendly packaging solutions, such as recyclable aluminum cans and biodegradable materials. The choice of packaging also influences the perception of quality; for many, cans are now seen as a premium option, offering better protection against light and oxygen, which can spoil beer.

Some breweries have even embraced unique packaging designs that enhance the overall experience. For example, limited-edition releases may come in specially designed bottles or cans adorned with intricate artwork, turning the packaging into a collectible item. This approach not only appeals to collectors but also adds an element of excitement and exclusivity.

The Role of Aesthetics in Consumer Experience

Ultimately, the aesthetic of beer—encompassing labels, logos, and packaging—plays a significant role in creating a narrative around the product. It influences how consumers perceive the quality and craftsmanship of a beer. In a world where consumers are becoming increasingly discerning, breweries that invest in thoughtful and creative aesthetics can differentiate themselves in a saturated market.

Moreover, the aesthetics of beer contribute to the overall social experience of enjoying a drink. Beer is often a communal experience, shared among friends at gatherings or festivals. Beautifully designed packaging can enhance the visual appeal of beer served in glasses, making it more Instagrammable and shareable on social media platforms. This visual culture around beer not only amplifies brand visibility but also fosters a sense of community among enthusiasts.

In conclusion, the aesthetic elements of beer—labels, logos, and packaging—are not just marketing tools; they are integral to the identity of breweries and the overall consumer experience. As the craft beer landscape continues to evolve, the importance of these visual components will only grow, reflecting the artistry and passion that brewers pour into their creations.

Beer and Festivals: Oktoberfest and Other Beer Celebrations

Beer has long been intertwined with celebrations and festivals across cultures, serving not just as a beverage but as a social catalyst that brings people together. Among the myriad of beer festivals worldwide, Oktoberfest stands out as the most famous, representing a rich tapestry of tradition, culture, and community engagement.

Oktoberfest: A Historical Overview

Oktoberfest originated in Munich, Germany, in 1810 as a royal wedding celebration for Crown Prince Ludwig and Princess Therese of Bavaria. The festivities included horse races, food stalls, and, of course, plenty of beer. Initially lasting for just a few days, the event proved so popular that it was expanded into an annual festival. Over the years, Oktoberfest has evolved into a 16- to 18-day extravaganza, typically running from late September to the first weekend in October, attracting millions of visitors from around the globe.

The festival is hosted at Theresienwiese, a large open space in Munich, where massive beer tents, amusement rides, and various attractions create a vibrant atmosphere. The beer served at Oktoberfest is traditionally brewed within the city limits of Munich and must adhere to the Reinheitsgebot, or German Beer Purity Law, which dictates the ingredients that can be used in beer production. The festival showcases a variety of beer styles, predominantly Märzen, a rich lager that is brewed in March and served throughout the festival.

The Cultural Significance of Beer Festivals

Beer festivals like Oktoberfest serve more than just a purpose of consumption; they encapsulate cultural heritage and community spirit. They offer a platform for local breweries to showcase their craft, providing attendees with a diverse range of beer styles and flavors. In addition to tasting unique brews, visitors indulge in traditional German cuisine such as pretzels, sausages, and schnitzels, further enhancing the gastronomic experience.

Beyond the culinary aspects, beer festivals often include music, dancing, and traditional attire, such as lederhosen and dirndls, promoting a sense of community and celebration of cultural identity. These elements combine to offer visitors an immersive experience that honors local customs while inviting international participation.

Other Notable Beer Celebrations

While Oktoberfest is the most recognized beer festival, numerous other celebrations around the world focus on beer, each with its unique flair. For instance, the Great American Beer Festival (GABF) in Denver, Colorado, is one of the largest beer festivals in the United States, celebrating the craft beer movement. It features thousands of beers from hundreds of breweries, along with educational seminars and tastings.

In Belgium, the Brussels Beer Weekend is an annual event that highlights the country's rich brewing traditions. Attendees can sample a wide variety of Belgian beers, including Trappist ales and lambics, while enjoying music and local culinary delights.

The UK hosts various beer festivals, including the Campaign for Real Ale (CAMRA) festivals, which focus on traditional cask ales and promote the appreciation of real ale brewing. These festivals, held across cities like London and Manchester, underscore the local beer culture and community involvement.

The Modern Beer Festival Experience

In recent years, beer festivals have expanded beyond traditional settings. Many cities host craft beer festivals that celebrate local breweries and the growing craft beer movement. These events often feature food trucks, live music, and artisan vendors, creating a festival atmosphere that appeals to a broader audience.

As beer festivals continue to evolve, they also embrace sustainability, incorporating eco-friendly practices and promoting local sourcing. This shift reflects a growing awareness of the environmental impact of beer production and consumption.

Conclusion

Beer festivals, exemplified by Oktoberfest, play a significant role in cultural expression and community bonding. They celebrate not just the beverage itself but the traditions, flavors, and innovations that come from brewing. As these festivals continue to grow in popularity across the globe, they remain vital to the social fabric of societies, fostering connections that transcend geographical boundaries.

Chapter 13

Beer in Modern Popular Culture

Beer in Film and Television: Iconic Moments

Beer has long held a prominent place in the cultural fabric of society, and its representation in film and television has significantly contributed to its status as a beloved beverage. The portrayal of beer in visual media often encapsulates not only the enjoyment of the drink but also the social interactions and cultural contexts surrounding it. From comedies to dramas, beer has served as both a narrative device and a symbol of camaraderie, celebration, and sometimes, excess.

One of the most iconic moments in film history involving beer is found in the 1978 comedy Animal House. This quintessential college film, which captures the reckless spirit of fraternity life, features a memorable scene where the character Bluto, played by John Belushi, famously chugs a beer while encouraging a crowd of rowdy students. This moment not only solidifies Bluto's reputation as the life of the party but also encapsulates the film's themes of youthful rebellion and the exuberance of college life. The imagery of beer in this context serves as a catalyst for fun, mischief, and the forging of friendships, becoming a cultural touchstone that resonates with audiences even decades later.

Television has also made significant contributions to the portrayal of beer, with shows like Cheers setting the gold standard. The Boston-based bar, where everybody knows your name, serves as more than just a backdrop; it is a character in its own right. The interactions between patrons over a pint highlight the social aspect of beer drinking. Iconic moments, such as the characters sharing their life stories or engaging in light-hearted banter across the bar, illustrate beer as a unifying force. The show's enduring popularity speaks to its ability to capture the essence of community, all centered around the act of sharing a beer.

Another notable example is the cult classic The Big Lebowski, where the character Jeff Lebowski, aka "The Dude," epitomizes a laid-back lifestyle heavily associated with beer consumption. The film's iconic "White Russian" cocktail may overshadow the beer, but it is the scenes of The Dude lounging with a beer in hand that illustrate a culture of relaxation and nonchalance. These moments resonate with viewers who appreciate the juxtaposition of beer's casual consumption against life's more profound dilemmas, capturing the spirit of the 1990s counterculture.

In more recent years, the representation of beer has evolved alongside changing societal attitudes. In the acclaimed series Parks and Recreation, Leslie Knope's love for local beer and her interactions with the quirky characters of Pawnee reflect a celebration of craft brewing and local breweries. The show often uses beer as a means to foster community spirit, highlight local businesses, and illustrate the importance of social gatherings. Iconic moments, such as the "Pawnee Commons" episode, where characters unite over a shared love for beer, illustrate how the beverage can be a vehicle for change and community development.

Beer in film and television has also been used to comment on social issues. In the gripping drama Breaking Bad, the character Walter White's descent into the criminal underworld is often juxtaposed with scenes of beer consumption, symbolizing both the mundane and the chaotic aspects of his life. Each beer shared can represent a moment of normalcy, which starkly contrasts with the underlying tension of his illegal activities.

Overall, beer's portrayal in film and television serves as a rich narrative device that reflects cultural values, social interactions, and individual character arcs. Iconic moments involving beer not only entertain but also provoke thought about the role of alcohol in society, the nature of friendship, and the celebration of life's milestones. As a symbol of community and camaraderie, beer will undoubtedly continue to find its place in the stories we tell and the moments we cherish on screen.

Beer and Sports

The relationship between beer and sports is a long-standing cultural phenomenon that transcends geographical boundaries and social classes. This connection is deeply rooted in tradition and has evolved into a multi-faceted partnership that plays a significant role in the sporting experience for millions around the world. Beer, often dubbed "the drink of champions," has become synonymous with sporting events, creating a unique synergy between athleticism and leisure.

Historically, the pairing of beer with sports can be traced back to ancient cultures. In ancient Greece, beer was consumed during athletic competitions such as the Olympic Games, where spectators would cheer on their favorites while enjoying a refreshing brew. Similarly, in ancient Rome, public baths and arenas were often filled with patrons who shared a common love for both sports and beer. These early instances of beer consumption during sports laid the groundwork for today's culture.

In modern times, the relationship between beer brands and sports has become increasingly commercialized. Major breweries often enter into sponsorship agreements with sporting events, teams, and leagues. These partnerships serve dual purposes: they provide financial support to the teams and events while simultaneously offering beer brands extensive exposure to target demographics. For instance, during the Super Bowl, one of the most-watched sporting events in the United States, beer brands invest heavily in advertising, creating memorable commercials that resonate with audiences. This strategy not only enhances brand recognition but also solidifies the association between beer and the excitement of sports.

Moreover, beer brands have embraced the concept of experiential marketing by creating interactive experiences at sporting events. Many breweries set up pop-up beer gardens, tasting tents, and promotional booths at stadiums and arenas, allowing fans to sample new products, meet brand ambassadors, and engage with fellow sports enthusiasts. These experiences often elevate the overall enjoyment of the event, fostering a sense of community among fans. For example, events like the annual Oktoberfest in Munich attract sports fans and beer lovers alike, merging the thrill of sporting competitions with the celebration of beer culture.

The relationship between beer and sports is also reflected in the design of sporting venues. Many stadiums and arenas now feature a wide array of craft and domestic beer options, catering to the diverse tastes of fans. The availability of localized brews has become a point of pride for many teams, allowing them to connect with their communities and support local breweries. This trend not only enhances the game-day experience but also contributes to the local economy, showcasing the intertwined nature of beer culture and sports.

Socially, beer has been recognized as a catalyst for camaraderie and celebration among fans. Whether it's sharing a pint with friends during a game or enjoying a cold one at a tailgate party, beer fosters connections and enhances the collective experience of sports. The rituals surrounding beer consumption during sports events—such as cheers, toasts, and shared moments of victory—create lasting memories and strengthen bonds among fans.

However, it's essential to acknowledge the responsibilities that come with this relationship. As the popularity of beer at sporting events continues to rise, so too does the need for responsible consumption. Many sporting venues and beer brands are now promoting initiatives that encourage moderation and responsible drinking, ensuring that the enjoyment of beer enhances the sporting experience rather than detracts from it.

In conclusion, the relationship between beer and sports is a rich tapestry woven from history, culture, and commerce. The synergy between these two realms has evolved into a powerful partnership that not only enhances the enjoyment of sporting events but also fosters community, supports local economies, and creates memorable experiences for fans worldwide.

As the world of sports continues to grow, so too will the significance of beer in this vibrant and dynamic environment.

The Rise of Beer Influencers on Social Media

In recent years, the landscape of beer marketing and consumption has undergone a significant transformation, largely driven by the rise of social media and the emergence of beer influencers. This phenomenon has reshaped how consumers discover, engage with, and enjoy beer, creating a vibrant community where enthusiasts share their passion and knowledge with a broader audience.

The Emergence of Beer Influencers

The term "beer influencer" refers to individuals who leverage social media platforms to promote beer culture, evaluate different brews, and connect with fellow beer lovers. These influencers come from various backgrounds, including professional brewers, craft beer enthusiasts, bloggers, and even casual drinkers with a keen eye for quality. Their rise can be attributed to the accessibility of social media platforms such as Instagram, YouTube, and TikTok, which allow for visual storytelling and direct engagement with followers.

Impact on Beer Culture

Beer influencers play a crucial role in shaping beer culture by providing insights into the world of brewing, tasting, and pairing. They often share reviews, tasting notes, and recommendations for various beer styles, breweries, and events. This democratization of beer knowledge allows consumers to make informed choices and fosters a sense of community among enthusiasts. By highlighting lesser-known breweries and unique beer styles, influencers also contribute to the diversification of beer culture, encouraging consumers to explore beyond popular brands.

Authenticity and Trust

One of the key factors behind the success of beer influencers is authenticity. Unlike traditional advertising, which may come across as disingenuous, influencers often build their followings through genuine passion and expertise. Their audiences tend to trust their opinions, as they share personal experiences and insights rather than scripted marketing messages. This trust translates into significant purchasing power, as followers are more likely to seek out beers recommended by influencers they admire.

The Role of Visual Content

Visual content is a cornerstone of social media, and beer influencers excel in creating appealing imagery that captures the essence of beer culture. High-quality photos and videos showcasing beer pours, brewery tours, and food pairings engage viewers and evoke a sensory experience.

This visual storytelling not only draws attention to specific beers but also enhances the overall appreciation of the craft. Platforms like Instagram have become virtual galleries for beer enthusiasts, where aesthetics play a significant role in influencing consumer preferences.

Collaborations with Breweries
As the influence of these social media personalities has grown, many breweries have recognized the potential of collaborating with influencers to promote their products. Influencer partnerships can take many forms, including sponsored posts, tasting events, and brewery takeovers. Such collaborations enable breweries to tap into the influencer's established audience, leading to increased visibility and sales. Furthermore, influencers often provide valuable feedback on new brews, helping breweries refine their offerings.

Challenges and Criticisms
Despite their positive contributions, the rise of beer influencers is not without challenges. The commercialization of influencer culture can lead to a dilution of authenticity, where some influencers may prioritize sponsored content over genuine passion for beer. Additionally, the sheer volume of influencers can create noise in the market, making it difficult for consumers to discern credible voices from those less knowledgeable.

Conclusion
The rise of beer influencers on social media marks a significant shift in the beer industry, where traditional marketing approaches are increasingly giving way to personal narratives and community engagement. These influencers not only educate consumers but also foster connections among beer lovers, enriching the overall culture surrounding beer. As the industry continues to evolve, the role of these influencers will likely remain pivotal in shaping consumer preferences and trends, ensuring that beer culture remains vibrant and accessible to all.

Beer Challenges and Trends: Viral Challenges and Beer Consumption

In the contemporary landscape of beer consumption, social media has become a powerful catalyst for trends, influencing how enthusiasts engage with beer culture. Among these trends, viral challenges have emerged as a significant phenomenon, shaping the social dynamics of beer drinking and fostering community interaction. These challenges often harness the power of platforms like TikTok, Instagram, and YouTube, where users share their own takes on popular drinking games, tastings, and creative consumption methods, contributing to a larger conversation about beer.

Understanding Viral Challenges

Viral challenges related to beer typically involve a specific activity or theme that encourages participants to showcase their creativity, skill, or humor. One of the most famous examples is the "Ice Bucket Challenge," which, while not exclusively about beer, inspired numerous adaptations that included beer drinking components. Other challenges, like the "Beer Mile," where participants drink a beer before each lap of a mile run, have gained traction in both competitive and casual drinking circles. Challenges like these not only promote engagement but also foster a sense of camaraderie among participants who share their experiences online.

The Role of Social Media

The rise of social media has drastically altered the landscape of beer consumption, facilitating the rapid spread of these challenges. Users often film themselves participating in challenges, adding a performative element that enhances the experience. This visibility encourages others to join in, creating a cascading effect that can lead to widespread participation across geographic boundaries. Platforms like TikTok, with its emphasis on short, catchy videos, have further amplified this trend, making it easy for users to create and share content that showcases their beer-related escapades.

Impact on Beer Culture

The viral nature of these challenges has had a transformative effect on beer culture. They not only promote experimentation with different beer styles but also encourage users to explore local breweries and craft beers. Challenges often highlight unique and obscure brews, prompting participants to seek out these options, thus supporting local businesses and diversifying their palates. Additionally, the playful and often humorous tone of these challenges can demystify beer consumption, making it more accessible to a broader audience, particularly younger drinkers who engage with these platforms.

Health and Safety Considerations

While many of these challenges promote social interaction and creativity, they also raise concerns regarding responsible drinking. The competitive nature of these challenges can sometimes lead to excessive consumption, overshadowing the importance of moderation. As a response, some influencers and organizations within the beer industry have begun advocating for responsible drinking practices, emphasizing the need to enjoy beer in a way that prioritizes health and safety.

The Future of Beer Challenges

Looking ahead, the trend of viral challenges in beer consumption is likely to evolve. As more consumers become health-conscious, challenges that promote low-alcohol or non-alcoholic beers may emerge, reflecting a shift towards moderation without sacrificing the social aspects of beer drinking. Additionally, as the craft beer movement continues to grow, challenges may increasingly focus on local breweries, seasonal offerings, and sustainability efforts, encouraging consumers to make choices that support their communities and the environment.

In conclusion, the intersection of beer challenges and viral trends illustrates the dynamic nature of beer consumption today. These challenges not only facilitate social bonding and community engagement but also reflect larger cultural shifts toward inclusivity, creativity, and responsible drinking. As the landscape of beer continues to evolve, so too will the ways in which enthusiasts engage with this age-old beverage, ensuring that the joy of beer remains a vibrant part of contemporary culture.

The Role of Advertising in Shaping Beer Culture

Advertising has been a powerful force in shaping consumer perceptions, preferences, and the overall culture surrounding beer. Since the inception of commercial brewing, advertising has evolved from simple word-of-mouth endorsements and signage to sophisticated marketing strategies that encompass print, television, radio, digital platforms, and social media. Each era of beer advertising has reflected the cultural values, technological advancements, and social trends of its time, contributing significantly to the identity of beer in society.

Historical Context

In the early days of beer production, advertisements were rudimentary, often relying on local gossip and community gatherings to spread the word about a brewer's offerings. However, as breweries grew in number and competition intensified, particularly in the 19th century, advertising began to take on a more formal role. Breweries started employing printed materials, such as posters and pamphlets, to reach broader audiences. The introduction of lithography allowed for colorful and eye-catching designs that helped distinguish one beer from another.

The late 19th and early 20th centuries saw the birth of brand identity in beer advertising. Slogans like "The King of Beers" and "Tastes Great, Less Filling" emerged, creating memorable phrases that resonated with consumers. These slogans not only aimed to promote specific brands but also sought to establish an emotional connection with the drinkers, embedding beer into the fabric of societal rituals and celebrations.

The Rise of Television and Modern Marketing

The advent of television revolutionized beer advertising. Commercials became a primary medium for breweries to convey their messages, often utilizing humor, celebrity endorsements, and evocative imagery to engage viewers. Iconic advertisements, like those featuring the Budweiser Clydesdales or Miller Lite's comedic skits, became ingrained in popular culture, creating a shared experience among consumers.

Moreover, advertising began to reflect and influence societal trends, such as the shift towards more casual drinking environments in the post-war era. Beer advertisements targeted younger audiences, promoting a lifestyle of fun, camaraderie, and leisure. This approach not only helped shape perceptions of beer as a social lubricant but also contributed to the normalization of beer consumption in various social settings, from backyard barbecues to sporting events.

Craft Beer and Niche Marketing

With the rise of the craft beer movement in the late 20th century, advertising underwent another transformation. Craft breweries often emphasized authenticity, local ingredients, and unique brewing methods, distinguishing themselves from mass-produced beers. Their marketing strategies leveraged storytelling and community engagement, appealing to consumers seeking more personalized and meaningful connections with their beverages.

Social media platforms have further reshaped the landscape of beer advertising in the 21st century. Craft breweries, in particular, have adeptly utilized platforms like Instagram and Facebook to showcase their creations, engage directly with consumers, and build loyal communities. Beer influencers and bloggers have emerged as significant players in the marketing space, often shaping trends and driving consumer interest through their recommendations and reviews.

Impacts on Society and Culture

The impact of beer advertising extends beyond mere sales figures; it shapes cultural perceptions of beer, identity, and social norms. Advertisements often reflect and reinforce stereotypes about gender, class, and lifestyle, influencing how consumers relate to beer. For example, traditional advertising has frequently portrayed beer as a masculine drink, while contemporary campaigns have begun to embrace a more diverse representation, acknowledging the growing role of women in the brewing industry and beer consumption.

Moreover, advertising campaigns often coincide with social movements, such as the push towards responsible drinking and sustainability. Many breweries now emphasize eco-friendly practices and community involvement in their marketing, appealing to environmentally-conscious consumers and fostering a culture of social responsibility.

In conclusion, advertising plays a crucial role in shaping beer culture, influencing consumer behavior, and reflecting societal changes. As the industry continues to evolve, so too will the strategies used to connect with drinkers, making beer advertising a dynamic and integral aspect of the beverage's history and future.

Chapter 14

The Science of Brewing

The Chemistry Behind Beer: Fermentation, Yeast, and Sugars

The production of beer is a complex interplay of chemistry and biology, primarily centered around the processes of fermentation, the role of yeast, and the contribution of sugars. Understanding these components is essential for brewers, as they dictate the flavor, aroma, and overall quality of the final product.

Fermentation

At its core, fermentation is a metabolic process that converts sugars into alcohol and carbon dioxide, facilitated by yeast. The chemical reaction can be summarized by the equation:

$$C_6H_{12}O_6 \rightarrow 2C_2H_5OH + 2CO_2$$

In this equation, glucose ($C_6H_{12}O_6$) is transformed into ethanol (C_2H_5OH) and carbon dioxide (CO_2). This process occurs in anaerobic conditions, meaning it takes place without oxygen. Yeast, primarily Saccharomyces cerevisiae for ales and Saccharomyces pastorianus for lagers, plays a pivotal role in this transformation.

Yeast cells consume sugars present in the wort (the liquid extracted from the malted grains), producing not just alcohol and CO_2, but also a variety of byproducts that contribute to the beer's flavor profile. These byproducts include esters, phenols, and higher alcohols, which can impart fruity, spicy, or floral notes to the beer.

Yeast: The Unsung Hero

Yeast is often regarded as the unsung hero of brewing. While it is a microorganism, its influence on beer is profound. Different strains of yeast exhibit distinct fermentation characteristics and flavor profiles, leading to a vast diversity of beer styles. For instance, ale yeast ferments at warmer temperatures, producing a rich array of esters and phenols, while lager yeast ferments at cooler temperatures, resulting in cleaner, crisper flavors.

Moreover, yeast must be managed carefully throughout the brewing process. Factors such as temperature, pH, and nutrient availability can significantly impact yeast health and performance. Stress factors can lead to off-flavors or incomplete fermentation, underscoring the delicate balance brewers must maintain.

Sugars: The Fuel of Fermentation
The sugars present in the brewing process originate primarily from malted barley, which is rich in starch. The malting process activates enzymes that convert these starches into fermentable sugars such as glucose, maltose, and dextrins.

During mashing, the malt is combined with hot water, allowing enzymes like amylase to break down the starches into simpler sugars. The resulting wort contains a mix of simple and complex sugars. Yeast preferentially ferments simple sugars like glucose and maltose, while complex sugars may remain unfermented, contributing to the beer's body and mouthfeel.

Sugar concentration plays a crucial role in determining the final alcohol content of the beer. Higher sugar levels lead to higher alcohol production, while lower sugar levels can yield a lighter beer. Additionally, the residual sugars after fermentation contribute to the sweetness and balance of the beer, which can be critical for styles such as IPAs or stouts, where the interplay of malt sweetness and hop bitterness is essential.

Conclusion
The chemistry behind beer is a fascinating blend of fermentation, yeast activity, and sugar manipulation. Each of these elements contributes to the unique characteristics of beer, from the flavor and aroma to the alcohol content and mouthfeel. Understanding this chemistry not only empowers brewers to create diverse beer styles but also enhances the appreciation of beer as a craft that marries science with art. As brewing technology advances, the exploration of yeast strains, sugar profiles, and fermentation techniques will continue to shape the future of beer, ensuring its place in both cultural and culinary contexts.

How Water Chemistry Affects Beer Styles
Water is often overlooked in discussions about beer, but it is a critical ingredient that significantly influences the flavor, aroma, and overall character of the finished product. The chemistry of water, particularly its mineral content, can alter the brewing process and result in distinct beer styles that reflect the region from which they originate.

The Basics of Water Chemistry
Water is made up of hydrogen and oxygen (H_2O), but its properties are greatly affected by the presence of various dissolved minerals and compounds. Key minerals found in brewing water include calcium, magnesium, sodium, sulfate, chloride, and bicarbonate. Each of these minerals

can enhance or suppress certain flavors in beer, depending on their concentrations and the balance between them.

1. Calcium: Primarily contributes to the overall hardness of the water. It helps with enzyme activity during mashing, aids in the precipitation of proteins, and enhances the mouthfeel of the beer. High levels of calcium can also accentuate hop bitterness and contribute to a clean finish.

2. Magnesium: Essential for yeast health and fermentation, magnesium can also impart a slight bitterness. However, excessive amounts can lead to off-flavors, making it crucial to maintain balanced levels.

3. Sodium: While often associated with a salty taste, small amounts of sodium can enhance the overall flavor profile of beer, especially in styles like porters and stouts. However, too much sodium can overpower the beer's other flavors.

4. Sulfate: Known for accentuating hop bitterness, sulfate can make pale ales and IPAs more crisp and dry. Higher sulfate levels are often desirable in styles that showcase hops, as they provide a clean finish that allows hop flavors to shine.

5. Chloride: In contrast to sulfate, chloride contributes to a fuller, rounder mouthfeel and can enhance malt sweetness. This mineral is beneficial in styles such as stouts and brown ales, where a luxurious mouthfeel is desirable.

6. Bicarbonate: Important for buffering the pH of brewing water, bicarbonate is essential for brewing darker beers like stouts and porters, where it helps to neutralize acidity. However, excessive bicarbonate can lead to a harsh taste, so careful management is necessary.

Regional Water Profiles and Their Impact on Beer Styles

Different geographical regions have distinct water profiles that have historically shaped local beer styles. For instance:

- **Burton-on-Trent, England:** Known for its high sulfate levels, the water from this region is ideal for brewing pale ales and IPAs, contributing to their distinctive bitterness and dry finish.

- **Munich, Germany:** The water in Munich is rich in chloride and bicarbonate, making it perfect for brewing malty beers like Hefeweizens and Märzen, which benefit from a smooth mouthfeel and a rich malt character.

- **Dublin, Ireland:** The soft water profile of Dublin is low in minerals, which is ideal for brewing stouts. It contributes to the creamy texture and enhances the roasted flavors characteristic of beers like Guinness.

The Modern Perspective: Adjusting Water Chemistry

With the advent of homebrewing and craft brewing, brewers now have the ability to adjust their water chemistry to suit the styles they want to produce. They can use water treatment techniques such as reverse osmosis, mineral additions, and dilution to create an ideal brewing water profile. This flexibility allows brewers to experiment and innovate, leading to a diverse array of beer styles that reflects not only traditional practices but also modern tastes.

In conclusion, water chemistry plays a foundational role in brewing, influencing everything from fermentation to the final flavor profile of the beer. Understanding and manipulating water chemistry allows brewers to create distinct styles that pay homage to regional traditions while pushing the boundaries of what is possible in craft beer production.

Innovations in Brewing Technology: Automated Brewing Systems

The brewing industry has undergone significant transformations since its inception, evolving from rudimentary methods of fermentation to the sophisticated processes of today. At the forefront of this evolution are automated brewing systems, which have revolutionized the way beer is produced, enhancing efficiency, consistency, and scalability. These technological advancements not only streamline operations but also allow brewers to focus more on creativity and quality.

The Genesis of Automation in Brewing

The automation of brewing processes began in the late 20th century, coinciding with the rise of industrial brewing. Traditional brewing was labor-intensive, requiring skilled artisans to monitor each step of the process, from mashing to fermentation. As demand for beer surged, particularly during the Industrial Revolution, breweries sought ways to increase output without sacrificing quality. Early innovations included the introduction of mechanical pumps and automated temperature controls, which laid the groundwork for more complex systems.

Components of Automated Brewing Systems

Modern automated brewing systems integrate a range of technologies to optimize various stages of production. The primary components of these systems include:

1. Programmable Logic Controllers (PLCs): These are digital computers used for automation of electromechanical processes. In brewing, PLCs control temperature, pressure, and timing, ensuring precise management of each brewing phase.

2. Sensors and Monitoring Equipment: Advanced sensors track critical parameters such as pH levels, specific gravity, and temperature throughout the brewing process. Real-time data collection allows brewers to make informed decisions quickly, adjusting variables to maintain consistency.

3. Automated Mashing Systems: Automated mash tuns can regulate temperature and timing with pinpoint accuracy. These systems allow for multiple mashing profiles to be programmed, accommodating different beer styles and recipes, which enhances flexibility and creativity.

4. Fermentation Control Systems: Automated fermentation tanks utilize temperature control and pressure monitoring to create optimal conditions for yeast activity. This not only improves fermentation efficiency but also leads to more predictable and desirable flavor profiles.

5. Data Management Software: Modern brewing systems often come equipped with software that tracks every aspect of production. This data can be analyzed to identify trends, optimize recipes, and enhance overall brewing performance.

Benefits of Automation

The shift towards automated brewing systems presents numerous advantages:

- Consistency and Quality: Automation reduces the variability inherent in manual brewing. With precise control over ingredients and processes, brewers can produce beer that consistently meets quality standards, fostering consumer trust and brand loyalty.

- Increased Efficiency: Automated systems can operate with minimal human intervention, allowing breweries to produce more beer in less time. This efficiency is particularly beneficial for larger operations or those looking to scale production without a corresponding increase in labor costs.

- Cost Savings: While the initial investment in automated systems can be significant, the long-term savings created by reduced labor costs, decreased material waste, and improved energy efficiency can be substantial. Additionally, better control over processes can lead to reduced ingredient costs.

- **Enhanced Innovation:** With routine tasks automated, brewers have more time to experiment with new recipes and techniques. This encourages creativity and innovation, driving the craft beer movement and leading to the development of unique and diverse beer styles.

Challenges of Implementation
Despite the numerous benefits, the transition to automated brewing systems is not without challenges. The upfront costs, technical complexity, and the need for staff training can be barriers for smaller breweries. Additionally, reliance on technology raises concerns about system failures and the potential loss of artisanal skills.

Conclusion
Automated brewing systems represent a significant leap forward in the brewing industry, marrying tradition with modern technology. As these systems continue to evolve, they promise to further enhance the brewing process, allowing brewers to focus on crafting exceptional beers while meeting the ever-increasing demand for diverse and high-quality products. The future of brewing is undoubtedly intertwined with technology, paving the way for a new era in beer production.

Yeast Strains and Their Influence on Flavor

Yeast is a fundamental ingredient in the brewing process, playing a crucial role in transforming the sugars derived from malted grains into alcohol and carbon dioxide through fermentation. However, beyond its basic function, yeast strains significantly influence the flavor and aroma profile of beer. Different strains of yeast each impart unique characteristics, leading to a diverse range of beer styles that are defined not only by the ingredients used but also by the fermentation process itself.

The Basics of Yeast in Brewing
Yeast is a living organism, a type of fungus, primarily belonging to the Saccharomyces cerevisiae species for ales and Saccharomyces pastorianus for lagers. These two categories of yeast are fundamental to the brewing world, as they operate under different fermentation conditions. Ales, fermented at warmer temperatures (60-75°F), tend to produce fruity and complex flavors, while lagers, fermented at cooler temperatures (45-55°F), generally yield cleaner and crisper profiles.

Flavor Compounds Produced by Yeast
During fermentation, yeast metabolizes sugars and produces a variety of byproducts, including alcohol, carbon dioxide, and a range of flavor compounds. These compounds include esters, phenols, and higher alcohols, which contribute to the beer's overall sensory experience.

- **Esters:** These are fruity and floral compounds that are often produced by yeast during fermentation. For example, the presence of isoamyl acetate can give a beer banana-like notes, while ethyl acetate might contribute a pear-like aroma. The specific strain of yeast used can greatly influence the type and concentration of esters produced.

- **Phenols:** These compounds can impart spicy or clove-like aromas, particularly in certain yeast strains such as those used in Belgian styles or wheat beers. For instance, the yeast strain used in brewing hefeweizen can produce significant amounts of phenolic compounds, leading to the signature clove and banana notes that characterize this style.

- **Higher Alcohols:** Also known as fusel alcohols, these compounds can add warmth and complexity to the beer's flavor. However, too high a concentration can lead to off-flavors. The production of higher alcohols is influenced by fermentation temperature, the health of the yeast, and the specific strain being used.

The Role of Yeast Selection

Brewers have a plethora of yeast strains to choose from, each with its own flavor profile and fermentation characteristics. The selection of a yeast strain is often driven by the desired outcome of the beer. For example, American ale yeast strains are known for their clean fermentation and are often used in IPAs to allow the hop flavors to shine through. Conversely, Belgian yeast strains are selected for their complex fruit and spice profiles, which can complement the malt backbone of the beer.

Fermentation Techniques and Yeast Management

In addition to the choice of yeast strain, fermentation techniques, and yeast management practices, such as temperature control and pitch rates, significantly impact the flavors produced during fermentation. High fermentation temperatures can enhance ester and phenol production, while lower temperatures can suppress these flavors, leading to a cleaner profile.

Moreover, the practice of "yeast wrangling"—the process of reusing and culturing yeast—allows brewers to develop distinctive house strains that can produce unique flavor profiles over time. By carefully managing the yeast, brewers can create consistency in their products while also experimenting with flavor variations.

Conclusion

The influence of yeast strains on beer flavor cannot be overstated. From the fruity esters of an American pale ale to the spicy phenols found in Belgian wits, the yeast used in brewing is pivotal in shaping the profile of the final product. As brewing science continues to advance, the exploration of new and traditional yeast strains will undoubtedly lead to further innovations and flavor discoveries in the ever-evolving world of beer.

Sustainable Brewing: Eco-Friendly Practices in the Beer Industry

Sustainable brewing has emerged as a critical focus within the beer industry as environmental awareness rises globally. Breweries are increasingly adopting eco-friendly practices to minimize their ecological footprint, conserve resources, and address the pressing challenges of climate change. This section delves into various sustainable practices that are redefining how beer is produced, distributed, and consumed.

1. Water Conservation:
Brewing is a water-intensive process, with estimates suggesting that it takes approximately 4-6 gallons of water to produce just one gallon of beer. To counteract this, many breweries are implementing water-saving technologies and practices. For instance, water reclamation systems are being used to recycle water from the brewing process, which can then be repurposed for cleaning or landscape irrigation. Innovations such as dry-hopping techniques also reduce water usage during the brewing process. Breweries are continually striving to improve their water-to-beer ratio, making strides toward more sustainable operations.

2. Energy Efficiency:
Breweries are significant energy consumers, and many are seeking ways to reduce their energy consumption and reliance on fossil fuels. The adoption of renewable energy sources, such as solar or wind power, is becoming increasingly common. Some breweries have installed solar panels on their facilities to generate clean energy, while others may purchase renewable energy credits to offset their carbon emissions. Additionally, energy-efficient brewing equipment, such as heat exchangers and energy recovery systems, helps to minimize energy use throughout the brewing process.

3. Waste Reduction:
Minimizing waste is a key component of sustainable brewing. Breweries generate a variety of byproducts, including spent grains, hops, and yeast. Many breweries are finding creative ways to repurpose these materials. For example, spent grains can be used as animal feed or as an ingredient in baked goods, while some breweries collaborate with local farms to utilize their byproducts in composting efforts. Additionally, initiatives to reduce packaging waste have gained traction, with many breweries opting for recyclable or biodegradable packaging materials. The push for a circular economy in brewing encourages the reuse and recycling of materials to reduce overall waste.

4. Sustainable Ingredients:
The sourcing of ingredients also plays a crucial role in sustainable brewing practices. Many breweries are choosing to use organic and locally sourced ingredients, which not only reduces the carbon footprint associated with transportation but also supports local agriculture. Additionally, some breweries are experimenting with alternative grains, such as millet or spelt, which require fewer resources to grow compared to traditional barley. This shift not only promotes biodiversity in agriculture but also encourages sustainable farming practices.

5. Community Engagement:
Sustainable brewing often extends beyond the brewery itself to include community involvement and education. Many breweries participate in local environmental initiatives, such as river cleanups or tree planting events, and host workshops to raise awareness about sustainability within their communities. By engaging with their customers and local stakeholders, breweries can foster a culture of sustainability and encourage responsible consumption among beer enthusiasts.

6. Certifications and Standards:
To further emphasize their commitment to sustainability, numerous breweries are pursuing certifications such as B Corporation Certification or LEED (Leadership in Energy and Environmental Design) accreditation. These certifications demonstrate adherence to rigorous environmental standards and show consumers that the brewery is dedicated to sustainable practices. As consumer demand for transparency and sustainability grows, breweries that adopt these standards can differentiate themselves in a competitive market.

In conclusion, sustainable brewing represents a paradigm shift in the beer industry, driven by a commitment to environmental stewardship and social responsibility. By embracing eco-friendly practices—ranging from water conservation and energy efficiency to waste reduction and sustainable sourcing—breweries are not only mitigating their impact on the planet but also appealing to a growing demographic of environmentally conscious consumers. As the industry continues to evolve, the integration of sustainability into brewing practices will undoubtedly shape the future of beer production worldwide.

Chapter 15

Beer and Gastronomy

The Art of Beer Pairing: Complementing Food with Beer

The art of beer pairing has gained significant attention in recent years, paralleling the rise of craft beer culture and an increased interest in culinary experiences. Much like wine pairing, the practice of matching specific beers with food enhances the flavors of both, creating a harmonious dining experience. Understanding the various components of beer and how they interact with different foods is crucial in mastering this art.

Understanding Beer Components

Beer is composed of several key ingredients: malt, hops, yeast, and water, each contributing unique flavors and aromas. The malt adds sweetness and body, while hops introduce bitterness and aromatic qualities. Yeast is responsible for fermentation and can impart fruity or spicy notes, depending on the strain used. Water chemistry also plays a role, influencing the beer's mouthfeel and overall taste profile. These components create a diverse range of beer styles, from light lagers to rich stouts, each with distinct characteristics.

Principles of Pairing

The general principles of beer pairing can be categorized into complementary and contrasting flavors. Complementary pairings involve matching similar flavor profiles, such as pairing a malty beer with caramelized dishes. For instance, a rich, amber ale can beautifully enhance the flavors of roasted meats or caramelized vegetables, as the maltiness echoes the sweetness of the food.

On the other hand, contrasting pairings highlight differences to create balance. A classic example is pairing a hoppy IPA with spicy foods. The bitterness of the beer can cut through the heat of the spices, providing a refreshing contrast that allows both the beer and the food to shine. Similarly, a tart Berliner Weisse can complement the richness of a creamy cheese, while its acidity cleanses the palate.

Beer Styles and Food Pairings

1. Lagers: These clean, crisp beers are versatile and can pair well with light dishes. A pilsner or a helles lager complements seafood, salads, and grilled chicken, enhancing the freshness of the ingredients.

2. Wheat Beers: With their fruity and spicy notes, wheat beers like Hefeweizen or Witbier pair excellently with salads, light pastas, and citrusy dishes. The refreshing qualities of these beers enhance the flavors without overwhelming them.

3. IPAs: Known for their hoppy bitterness, IPAs shine alongside spicy foods such as Thai or Indian cuisine. The hops can cut through the richness of creamy sauces, making for a balanced meal.

4. Stouts and Porters: Rich and robust, these dark beers are ideal for pairing with hearty dishes. They work well with grilled meats, chocolate desserts, or even barbecued ribs, as their bold flavors complement and enhance the umami elements in the food.

5. Sours: Tart beers such as Gose or Lambic can add an exciting twist to pairings. They are excellent with tangy cheeses, salads with vinaigrette dressings, or even dishes featuring pickled ingredients.

Pairing Beyond the Plate
Beer pairing isn't limited to food; it extends to the entire dining experience. Craft beer dinners, where chefs and brewers collaborate to create multi-course meals with specific beer pairings, have become increasingly popular. These events allow diners to explore the depth of flavors that can be achieved through thoughtful pairings, turning a meal into a memorable occasion.

Conclusion
The art of beer pairing is an evolving practice that invites experimentation and creativity. As the craft beer movement continues to grow, so too does the appreciation for the complex relationships between food and beer. Whether in a casual setting or a fine dining experience, understanding the principles of pairing can elevate the enjoyment of both food and beer, creating a symphony of flavors that delights the palate. Embracing this art not only enriches culinary experiences but also fosters a deeper connection to the diverse world of beer.

Cooking with Beer: Traditional and Modern Recipes
Cooking with beer is a culinary practice that has been embraced across cultures for centuries, infusing dishes with complex flavors and aromas that elevate a meal. Beer's diverse range of styles—from light lagers to rich stouts—allows for creativity in the kitchen, pairing with ingredients to create both traditional and contemporary recipes.

Traditional Uses of Beer in Cooking
Historically, beer has been utilized in various cuisines as a key ingredient in stews, marinades, and baking. In Belgian cuisine, for instance, dishes like Carbonnade Flamande, a hearty beef stew, rely on dark ales to impart a rich depth of flavor. The beer serves to tenderize the meat while contributing a distinct caramel sweetness that balances the savory elements of the dish.

Similarly, in German cooking, beer is often used in recipes such as Sauerbraten, a pot roast that is marinated in a mixture of beer, vinegar, and spices, creating a flavor profile that is both tangy and robust.

Beer batter is another traditional method of incorporating beer into cooking, particularly in the preparation of fried foods. The carbonation in beer creates a light and crispy texture, seen in classics like fish and chips or beer-battered onion rings. The choice of beer can affect the flavor of the batter; for example, using a pale ale will yield a different taste compared to a stout, which adds a hint of chocolate or coffee notes.

Modern Culinary Innovations
In contemporary kitchens, chefs have embraced beer not only for its flavor but also for its versatility in pairing with various types of cuisine. Craft beer's explosion in popularity has opened up new avenues for creativity, leading to innovative recipes that transcend traditional boundaries. One example is beer-infused barbecue sauces, where a hoppy IPA can be combined with tomatoes, brown sugar, and spices to create a sauce that layers flavor on grilled meats.

Baking with beer has also gained traction, with recipes for beer bread becoming commonplace. The yeast in beer contributes to the leavening process, resulting in a moist loaf that can be flavored with herbs, cheese, or even bacon. A simple recipe involves mixing equal parts of self-rising flour and a light beer, such as a lager, along with seasonings. The result is a quick bread that pairs beautifully with soups or can be enjoyed on its own.

Beer in Desserts
Beyond savory dishes, beer is making its way into desserts, with recipes that highlight the unique flavors of different beer styles. For example, chocolate stout cake is a popular modern dessert that uses stout beer to enhance the richness of the chocolate. The beer adds moisture and depth, often complemented by coffee or vanilla, creating a decadent treat that pairs well with a scoop of ice cream.

Another innovative dessert is beer ice cream, which can be crafted by incorporating beer into a traditional ice cream base. The alcohol content in beer helps to keep the ice cream creamy and smooth while imparting complex flavors that can range from fruity to malty, depending on the type of beer used.

Conclusion
Cooking with beer presents an exciting opportunity to explore culinary traditions and innovate new recipes. From stews and marinades to baked goods and desserts, beer enhances dishes with its unique flavors, making it a versatile ingredient in both traditional and modern cooking. As the craft beer movement continues to grow, so too does the potential for culinary creativity,

encouraging home cooks and professional chefs alike to experiment and discover new ways to incorporate this beloved beverage into their kitchens. Whether enjoying a hearty meal or a decadent dessert, beer can transform the dining experience, proving that it is much more than just a drink.

Beer and Cheese Pairing: A Guide for Enthusiasts

Pairing beer with cheese is a time-honored culinary tradition that enhances the flavors of both components, creating a delightful sensory experience. The complex profiles of beers and cheeses can interact harmoniously, highlighting the unique characteristics of each. This guide explores the principles of beer and cheese pairing, offering tips and suggestions for enthusiasts looking to elevate their tasting experiences.

Understanding Flavor Profiles

To achieve a successful pairing, it is essential to understand the flavor profiles of both beer and cheese. Beer can be categorized into various styles—such as lagers, ales, stouts, and IPAs—each bringing distinct flavors, aromas, and textures. Similarly, cheese varieties range from soft and creamy to hard and crumbly, with flavors that can be mild, tangy, or nutty.

When pairing beer and cheese, consider the following fundamental principles:

1. Complementarity: Pair beers and cheeses with similar flavor notes. For instance, a rich, malty stout can beautifully complement a creamy blue cheese, as both share deep, intense flavors.

2. Contrast: Sometimes, contrasting flavors can create a delightful tension on the palate. A sharp cheddar may be paired with a refreshing, citrusy IPA, where the bitterness of the beer cuts through the richness of the cheese.

3. Intensity: Match the intensity of the beer with that of the cheese. Stronger cheeses, like aged Gouda or Roquefort, require robust beers, such as barleywines or imperial stouts, to balance their flavors.

4. Regional Pairings: Consider pairing beers and cheeses from the same region. For example, a Belgian Dubbel pairs wonderfully with Belgian Trappist cheeses, both of which share similar fermentation traditions and flavor profiles.

Classic Pairing Suggestions
Here are some classic pairings to inspire your exploration:

- **Pale Ale and Cheddar:** The hoppy bitterness of a pale ale complements the nutty, sharp flavors of aged cheddar. This pairing is ideal for a casual gathering, as both elements are crowd-pleasers.

- **Wheat Beer and Brie:** The light, fruity notes of a hefeweizen or witbier harmonize with the creamy texture and subtle flavors of Brie. This pairing works well for summer picnics or light appetizers.

- **Porter and Blue Cheese:** The dark, roasted malt flavors of a porter enhance the pungent, salty characteristics of blue cheese. This combination is perfect for those who appreciate bold flavors.

- **Saison and Goat Cheese:** The earthy, herbal notes of a saison can elevate the tangy, creamy profile of fresh goat cheese. This pairing is delightful for springtime gatherings.

Tips for Pairing

1. Experiment: Personal taste plays a significant role in pairing. Don't be afraid to experiment with different combinations to discover what you enjoy most.

2. Serving Temperature: Serve beer and cheese at the appropriate temperatures. Cheeses are typically best served at room temperature, while beers should be chilled to enhance their refreshing qualities.

3. Presentation: Consider presenting your pairings on a wooden board with garnishes like fruits, nuts, or honey. This not only enhances the aesthetic appeal but also adds complementary flavors to the tasting experience.

4. Tasting Order: When sampling multiple pairings, start with lighter beers and cheeses, gradually moving to more robust combinations. This prevents the stronger flavors from overshadowing the more delicate ones.

Conclusion
Beer and cheese pairing is an art that invites creativity and personal expression. By understanding the principles of flavor synergy and experimenting with different styles, enthusiasts can create memorable tasting experiences. Whether hosting a gathering or enjoying a quiet evening at home, the delightful marriage of beer and cheese awaits to be explored.

Beer Dinners: Multi-Course Meals with Beer Pairings

Beer dinners have emerged as a celebrated culinary trend that highlights the versatility and complexity of beer as a gastronomic companion. This dining experience involves a carefully curated multi-course meal, where each dish is paired with specific beers chosen to enhance the flavors of the food, offering a unique palate experience that can rival traditional wine pairings.

The Concept of Beer Pairing

At the heart of beer dinners is the principle of pairing: selecting beers that either complement or contrast the flavors of the dishes being served. This not only elevates the meal but also showcases the diverse characteristics of different beer styles, from hoppy IPAs to rich stouts. The goal is to create a harmonious balance where the flavors of the food and beer amplify one another, leading to a more profound dining experience.

Structure of a Beer Dinner

Typically, a beer dinner consists of several courses—usually three to five—each accompanied by a different beer. The courses can range from appetizers to desserts, allowing chefs to demonstrate their culinary creativity while encouraging beer enthusiasts to explore various styles and flavors. For example, a typical structure might include:

1. Starter Course: Light and refreshing beers such as lagers or wheat beers paired with salads or seafood.
2. Main Course: Rich, full-bodied beers like amber ales or porters served alongside heartier dishes, such as grilled meats or rich stews.
3. Cheese Course: A selection of artisanal cheeses paired with a variety of beers that highlight their distinct flavors—think a sharp cheddar with an IPA or a creamy brie with a Belgian ale.
4. Dessert Course: Sweet stouts or fruit beers served with desserts, such as chocolate cake or fruit tarts, creating a delightful conclusion to the meal.

The Role of the Chef and Brewer

In a successful beer dinner, collaboration between the chef and the brewer is paramount. Chefs often work closely with brewers to understand the nuances of each beer, ensuring that the chosen pairings are not merely coincidental but rather the result of thoughtful consideration. Many establishments invite local craft breweries to participate, fostering a sense of community and supporting local businesses.

Educational Component

Beer dinners also serve an educational purpose. Many events feature a guided tasting component where the chef or brewer discusses the characteristics of each beer, the reasons behind its pairing, and any unique brewing techniques that might enhance the understanding of the beer's flavor profile. This interactive element deepens attendees' appreciation for the intricacies of beer and its potential in culinary applications.

Trends and Innovations
As the craft beer movement continues to grow, beer dinners are becoming more innovative. Some events focus on specific themes, such as regional beers, seasonal ingredients, or even pairing beers with international cuisines. Additionally, chefs are experimenting with cooking techniques that incorporate beer into the dishes themselves, infusing sauces or marinades with beer, which can further enhance the dining experience.

Conclusion
Beer dinners represent a dynamic intersection of culinary art and brewing craftsmanship, inviting diners to explore the potential of beer beyond its traditional role as a beverage. With the right pairings, a multi-course meal can transform into a celebration of flavors, showcasing the versatility of beer as an essential component of modern gastronomy. As the world of craft beer continues to evolve, so too will the possibilities for beer dinners, ensuring that they remain a vibrant part of the culinary landscape.

The Role of Beer in Fine Dining: How Top Chefs Use Beer in Menus
In recent years, the culinary landscape has evolved dramatically, with beer emerging as a versatile and sophisticated ingredient in fine dining. Top chefs are increasingly recognizing the potential of beer not just as a beverage but as a key component in crafting innovative dishes. This shift can be attributed to a growing appreciation of beer's complex flavors, its diverse styles, and the cultural significance it holds across various cuisines.

Elevating Traditional Pairings
Traditionally, wine has been the go-to beverage for pairing with gourmet meals, but chefs are now embracing beer's unique flavor profiles to complement food in exciting ways. Beer's carbonation, bitterness, sweetness, and acidity can enhance the taste of a dish, much like wine. For instance, a rich, creamy dish such as risotto can be beautifully paired with a hoppy IPA that cuts through the creaminess and elevates the overall flavor experience. Similarly, stouts with their roasted malt characteristics can enhance the depth of chocolate desserts, creating a harmonious balance between sweet and bitter elements.

Cooking with Beer
Beyond pairing, chefs are incorporating beer directly into their cooking techniques. Beer can be used as a marinade, providing tenderization and flavor infusion, particularly in meats such as pork and chicken. For instance, a marinade made with a malty brown ale can impart a caramelized sweetness to grilled meats. Additionally, beer can be utilized in sauces, soups, and

stews, where it can add depth and complexity. A classic example is the use of Belgian ale in a rich beef stew, where the beer contributes to the dish's umami character.

Crafting Signature Dishes

Many chefs are developing signature dishes that highlight specific beer styles, demonstrating their creativity and understanding of flavor compatibility. This trend is particularly evident in gastropubs and fine dining establishments alike, where chefs might create a beer-braised short rib dish, served alongside a pale ale reduction, or a beer-infused cheese sauce accompanying artisanal pretzels. By spotlighting local and craft breweries, chefs are also fostering community connections and promoting regional flavors, which resonate with diners increasingly interested in the provenance of their food and drink.

Beer Tastings and Pairing Events

In the fine dining realm, beer has also found its place in curated tasting menus and pairing events. Chefs are collaborating with local breweries to craft multi-course meals that feature beer pairings for each course. These events allow diners to explore the intricate relationships between food and beer in a structured format, enhancing their dining experience. For example, a seafood dish might be paired with a crisp, refreshing lager, while a dessert featuring fruit could be complemented by a fruity lambic, showcasing the versatility of beer across courses.

The Aesthetic of Beer in Fine Dining

Presentation also plays a crucial role in the integration of beer into fine dining. Glassware designed specifically for different beer styles enhances the visual appeal and overall experience. Chefs often take great care in selecting the appropriate glass for serving beer, as its shape can influence aroma and flavor perception. Innovative serving techniques, such as beer floats or beer-infused ice creams, further demonstrate the potential for creativity that beer brings to the table.

Conclusion

The role of beer in fine dining is rapidly evolving, as top chefs harness its unique qualities to create memorable culinary experiences. By pairing beer with food, cooking with it, and crafting signature dishes, they are redefining the relationship between food and beverage. As beer's reputation continues to grow within the culinary world, it is clear that this age-old beverage is not just a casual drink but a sophisticated ingredient worthy of a place on the fine dining table.

Chapter 16

The Future of Beer

The Impact of Climate Change on Beer Production
Climate change poses significant challenges to the production of beer, a beloved beverage with deep historical roots and cultural significance. As global temperatures rise, precipitation patterns shift, and extreme weather events become more frequent, the brewing industry faces a multitude of threats that can affect every stage of the brewing process, from the cultivation of raw ingredients to the fermentation and aging of beer.

1. Impact on Barley Production
Barley, the primary grain used in beer production, is particularly sensitive to climate variabilities. Optimal barley growth requires specific temperature ranges and consistent rainfall. Rising temperatures can lead to heat stress in barley crops, which may result in reduced yields and lower quality grains. Moreover, changes in precipitation patterns can lead to either drought conditions or excessive rainfall, both of which can adversely affect barley health. Drought can limit water availability for irrigation, while excessive moisture can lead to fungal diseases, ultimately compromising the grain's quality and, consequently, the beer produced from it.

2. Water Resources and Quality
Water is the most essential ingredient in beer, making up approximately 90% of its content. Climate change can significantly alter the availability and quality of freshwater resources. As regions experience prolonged droughts, the competition for water among agricultural, industrial, and municipal users intensifies. Additionally, increased rainfall can lead to flooding, affecting the infrastructure needed for water collection and treatment. Changes in water temperature can also impact the brewing process, as yeast activity is sensitive to such fluctuations. Breweries may need to invest in advanced water management systems to ensure a consistent supply of high-quality water.

3. Yeast Fermentation Dynamics
Yeast, the microorganism responsible for fermentation, is also affected by climate change. Different yeast strains have varying tolerance levels to temperature fluctuations. Warmer fermentation temperatures can lead to off-flavors and altered aromas in beer, impacting the final product's quality. Brewers may find themselves needing to adapt their fermentation

practices, selecting yeast strains that are more resilient to changing conditions or modifying processes to maintain optimal fermentation environments.

4. Sourcing Ingredients
As climate change impacts traditional growing regions, breweries may need to source ingredients from new areas, which can lead to increased transportation costs and a potential loss of regional character in beers. For instance, areas previously known for high-quality barley may become unsuitable for cultivation, forcing brewers to explore alternative grain sources. This shift can result in variations in flavor profiles and may challenge the identity of certain beer styles deeply tied to specific geographic locations.

5. Economic Considerations
The economic implications of climate change on beer production are profound. Increased costs associated with sourcing quality ingredients, water management, and adapting brewing processes can lead to higher prices for consumers. Additionally, smaller craft breweries, which may lack the financial resources of large corporations, could face greater challenges in adapting to these changes. This economic pressure might lead to market consolidation, with larger breweries acquiring struggling smaller ones, potentially stifling innovation and diversity within the beer market.

6. Sustainability Initiatives
In response to these challenges, many breweries are taking proactive steps toward sustainability. Initiatives include investing in renewable energy sources, implementing water conservation practices, and sourcing ingredients from sustainable farms. The rise of organic and biodynamic beer reflects a growing consumer demand for environmentally friendly practices. Breweries are increasingly recognizing their role not only in producing beer but also in advocating for environmental stewardship and climate resilience.

In conclusion, climate change presents a complex and multifaceted challenge to the beer production industry. As the effects of climate change become more pronounced, it will be crucial for breweries to adapt and innovate to ensure the continued enjoyment and accessibility of beer for future generations. By embracing sustainability and exploring new approaches to brewing, the industry can work towards mitigating the impacts of climate change while preserving the rich heritage and culture surrounding beer.

Technological Innovations in Brewing: The Use of AI
The brewing industry, steeped in tradition and historical practices, is undergoing a significant transformation with the integration of advanced technologies, particularly artificial intelligence

(AI). This innovation is reshaping how beer is produced, marketed, and consumed, leading to enhanced efficiency, quality, and creativity in brewing processes. AI's role in brewing is multifaceted, encompassing everything from recipe development to quality control and customer engagement.

Recipe Development and Optimization

One of the most exciting applications of AI in brewing is its potential to assist in the creation and optimization of beer recipes. Traditional brewing often relies on empirical methods and historical knowledge passed down through generations. However, AI can analyze vast amounts of data, including ingredient profiles, fermentation conditions, and historical brewing outcomes, to identify patterns and predict the sensory characteristics of different beer styles. Machine learning algorithms can suggest ingredient combinations that may yield unique flavors or improve existing recipes, thus enabling brewers to innovate while minimizing the risk of failure. This data-driven approach allows for experimentation with unconventional ingredients and brewing techniques, pushing the boundaries of what beer can be.

Quality Control and Consistency

Maintaining quality and consistency in beer production is paramount for breweries, especially as they scale up operations. AI can streamline quality control processes by monitoring various parameters throughout the brewing cycle, such as temperature, pH, and specific gravity. Sensors integrated with AI systems can collect real-time data, which can then be analyzed to detect anomalies or deviations from established norms. This predictive capability not only helps in identifying potential issues before they escalate but also ensures that each batch meets the desired specifications. By implementing AI-driven quality assurance protocols, breweries can enhance their product consistency, which is vital for building consumer trust and loyalty.

Supply Chain Management

AI's impact extends beyond the brewery floor; it also plays a crucial role in optimizing supply chain management. By analyzing historical sales data, market trends, and seasonal demand patterns, AI can forecast ingredient needs and manage inventory levels more effectively. This predictive analytics capability allows breweries to reduce waste, streamline procurement processes, and ensure that they have the necessary materials on hand when demand spikes. Additionally, AI can assist in logistics by optimizing delivery routes and schedules, further enhancing efficiency in the supply chain.

Customer Engagement and Marketing

In today's competitive market, understanding consumer preferences is essential for breweries to succeed. AI can analyze consumer data from various sources, including social media, reviews, and sales patterns, to identify emerging trends and preferences. This information can inform marketing strategies, product development, and promotional campaigns tailored to specific audience segments. Moreover, AI-driven chatbots and recommendation systems enhance customer engagement, providing personalized experiences and fostering a deeper connection between consumers and brands. By leveraging AI in marketing, breweries can respond more adeptly to consumer needs and preferences, ultimately driving sales and brand loyalty.

Sustainable Brewing Practices
As breweries increasingly focus on sustainability, AI can play a pivotal role in minimizing resource consumption and waste generation. For instance, machine learning algorithms can optimize energy use during the brewing process, recommend water-saving measures, and enhance waste management practices. By analyzing data on resource usage, AI can identify areas for improvement, leading to more eco-friendly brewing operations.

Conclusion
The integration of AI in brewing signifies a revolutionary shift in an industry that has long valued tradition. While the art of brewing remains central to the craft, the incorporation of advanced technologies is enabling brewers to innovate, improve quality, and enhance customer engagement. As the brewing industry continues to evolve, the fusion of tradition and technology promises to yield exciting new possibilities for beer enthusiasts and producers alike, paving the way for a future where creativity and efficiency coexist harmoniously.

The Growth of Non-Alcoholic Beer
In recent years, the beer industry has witnessed a significant shift in consumer preferences, leading to a remarkable growth in the non-alcoholic beer segment. No longer relegated to the fringes of the beverage market, non-alcoholic beer has emerged as a viable and appealing alternative for those seeking the taste of beer without the effects of alcohol. This transformation can be attributed to several factors, including changing societal attitudes towards alcohol consumption, health and wellness trends, and advancements in brewing technology.

Changing Attitudes Toward Alcohol
The cultural landscape surrounding alcohol consumption has evolved dramatically, particularly among younger generations. Increasingly, consumers are prioritizing health and well-being over traditional drinking norms. This shift is reflected in the rise of the "mindful drinking" movement, which encourages individuals to be more conscious of their alcohol intake. As a result, non-alcoholic beer has become an attractive option for those who wish to enjoy social experiences without the negative consequences associated with alcohol consumption, such as impaired judgment and hangovers.

Moreover, a growing awareness of the health risks linked to excessive drinking, including liver disease and addiction, has catalyzed a reevaluation of drinking habits. Non-alcoholic beer offers a way for consumers to partake in social settings while maintaining a healthier lifestyle, leading to increased demand across various demographics.

Health and Wellness Trends

The wellness trend has permeated all aspects of consumer behavior, influencing choices in food and beverage options. Non-alcoholic beer fits seamlessly into this trend, as it typically contains fewer calories and lower carbohydrates than its alcoholic counterparts. Many brands have started marketing their non-alcoholic beers as healthier alternatives, highlighting benefits such as hydration and the absence of hangover effects. This positioning aligns with consumers' desires for guilt-free indulgence and reinforces the appeal of non-alcoholic options.

Furthermore, the growth of the fitness culture has contributed to the rise of non-alcoholic beer. Many individuals who lead active lifestyles seek beverages that complement their health-conscious choices without sacrificing flavor. Non-alcoholic beers are now often found at gyms, fitness events, and health-focused restaurants, affirming their acceptance in diverse settings.

Advancements in Brewing Technology

The evolution of non-alcoholic beer can also be attributed to significant advancements in brewing technology. Traditional methods of producing non-alcoholic beer often resulted in products that were lacking in flavor and complexity. However, modern techniques have allowed brewers to create high-quality non-alcoholic beers that rival their alcoholic counterparts in taste and mouthfeel.

New brewing methods, such as vacuum distillation and reverse osmosis, enable brewers to extract alcohol from beer while preserving essential flavors and aromas. These innovations have led to a broader range of non-alcoholic beer styles, including IPAs, stouts, and lagers, appealing to a wide variety of palates. As craft breweries continue to experiment with flavors and styles, the non-alcoholic beer market is becoming increasingly sophisticated.

Market Expansion and Brand Innovation

The growth of non-alcoholic beer has not gone unnoticed by major breweries and craft producers alike. Many established brands have expanded their portfolios to include non-alcoholic options, recognizing the potential for profit in this burgeoning market. Additionally, new brands dedicated solely to non-alcoholic brewing have emerged, further diversifying the options available to consumers.

Marketing strategies have also evolved to target a broader audience, emphasizing the social aspects of non-alcoholic beer consumption. Campaigns often highlight the inclusivity of non-alcoholic beer, promoting it as a drink for everyone—whether for designated drivers, pregnant women, or individuals simply choosing to abstain from alcohol.

In summary, the growth of non-alcoholic beer represents a significant trend in the beverage industry, driven by changing societal attitudes, health and wellness trends, advancements in brewing technology, and market innovation. As consumers continue to seek out flavorful, low-alcohol alternatives, the non-alcoholic beer segment is likely to expand further, shaping the future of beer consumption worldwide.

Sustainability in Beer Production: Reducing Water and Energy Usage

The brewing industry, while steeped in tradition and creativity, faces increasing scrutiny regarding its environmental impact, particularly concerning resource consumption. The sustainability of beer production has become a pressing concern, with brewers seeking innovative methods to reduce water and energy usage while maintaining quality and efficiency. This section explores the various strategies and technologies adopted by breweries to achieve these goals.

Water Consumption: A Critical Challenge

Water is the most significant ingredient in beer, making up approximately 90% of its composition. However, the brewing process is notoriously water-intensive, with estimates suggesting that producing one liter of beer can require between three to ten liters of water, depending on the efficiency of the brewing process. As water scarcity becomes a global issue, many breweries are prioritizing water conservation techniques.

One effective method employed by breweries is the implementation of closed-loop water systems. These systems capture and recycle water used during the brewing process, including rinsing and cooling stages. By treating and reusing water, breweries can significantly reduce their overall water consumption. For example, some breweries have reported reductions of up to 50% in water usage by recycling water for cleaning and other non-potable purposes.

Additionally, advancements in technology have enabled brewers to monitor and manage their water usage more effectively. Smart sensors and data analytics allow for real-time tracking of water consumption, helping breweries identify areas of waste and implement corrective measures. By utilizing these technologies, brewers not only conserve water but also save on costs associated with water procurement and treatment.

Energy Efficiency: Brewing with Less

The brewing process is also energy-intensive, requiring substantial amounts of electricity and heat for boiling, fermentation, and refrigeration. To address these energy demands, many breweries are investing in energy-efficient technologies and practices that minimize their carbon footprint.

One prominent approach is the adoption of renewable energy sources. Breweries are increasingly turning to solar panels, wind turbines, and biomass systems to power their operations. For instance, some craft breweries have installed solar arrays that provide a significant portion of their energy needs, further reducing reliance on fossil fuels. This shift not only lowers greenhouse gas emissions but can also stabilize energy costs in the long run.

In addition to renewable energy, breweries are focusing on improving the efficiency of their equipment. Upgrading to energy-efficient boilers, refrigeration units, and lighting systems can yield substantial energy savings. Moreover, heat recovery systems capture excess heat generated during brewing and fermentation processes, repurposing it to preheat water or maintain optimal temperatures, thus reducing the energy required for heating.

Sustainable Practices Beyond Production

Sustainability in beer production extends beyond water and energy usage; it encompasses a holistic approach to environmentally responsible brewing. Many breweries are adopting sustainable practices in sourcing ingredients, packaging, and waste management. For example, utilizing locally sourced grains and hops not only reduces transportation emissions but also supports local agriculture.

Breweries are also exploring innovative packaging alternatives to minimize waste. The use of biodegradable materials, lightweight bottles, and recyclable cans can significantly reduce the environmental impact of packaging. Additionally, initiatives like deposit return schemes for bottles and cans encourage responsible recycling among consumers.

In waste management, many breweries are now employing methods to repurpose byproducts from the brewing process. Spent grains, a byproduct of brewing, are often donated to local farms as animal feed or utilized in the production of biofuels, thus contributing to a circular economy.

Conclusion

The movement towards sustainability in beer production is not merely a trend; it reflects a growing awareness of the environmental challenges facing the planet. By adopting water and energy reduction strategies, breweries can mitigate their impact on natural resources while fostering a culture of sustainability. As consumers increasingly seek environmentally friendly products, breweries that prioritize these practices will not only contribute to a healthier planet but may also gain a competitive edge in the market. Embracing sustainability is not just a responsibility; it is a pathway toward a more resilient and innovative brewing industry.

New Frontiers: Experimentation with Ingredients and Styles

The world of beer has undergone a remarkable transformation in recent years, particularly with the rise of craft brewing and the increased consumer demand for innovative flavors and styles. As brewers experiment with new ingredients and creative techniques, they are pushing the boundaries of what beer can be, resulting in an exciting renaissance of flavors and experiences that appeal to an ever-diversifying audience.

One of the most significant trends in modern brewing is the exploration of unconventional ingredients. Traditional beer is primarily made from malted barley, hops, water, and yeast. However, contemporary brewers are increasingly incorporating a variety of adjuncts such as fruit, spices, herbs, and even unusual items like coffee, chocolate, and tea. For instance, some brewers craft fruit-infused IPAs, blending the hoppy bitterness with the sweetness and tartness of fruits like mango, passionfruit, or raspberry. This experimentation not only creates unique flavor profiles but also caters to consumers' tastes for freshness and novelty.

Moreover, the use of alternative grains is gaining traction. While barley remains the primary grain for brewing, brewers are exploring options like wheat, rye, oats, and even gluten-free grains such as sorghum and millet. This shift toward alternative grains allows for a broader range of textures and flavors, contributing to the complexity of the final product. For example, rye can introduce a spiciness that complements certain beer styles, while oats can add a creamy mouthfeel, enhancing stouts and porters.

In addition to experimenting with ingredients, brewers are also innovating with brewing techniques. One notable method is barrel aging, where beers are aged in previously used barrels, often from spirits like bourbon or wine. This process infuses the beer with additional flavors from the wood and the residual contents of the barrel, creating rich and complex brews. Some brewers have taken this a step further by blending different barrel-aged beers to achieve a desired flavor profile, showcasing the art of blending as a crucial element of modern brewing.

Another frontier in brewing is the utilization of wild yeast strains and bacteria, which impart unique flavors and aromas to the beer. This approach, often associated with sour beers and lambics, embraces the natural fermentation process, resulting in complex flavors that can be both tart and funky. The use of Brettanomyces, a wild yeast, can create earthy and fruity characteristics that challenge traditional notions of beer flavor.

The rise of the craft beer movement has also led brewers to engage with local and seasonal ingredients. Many craft breweries are now focusing on sustainability by sourcing ingredients from local farms and using seasonal produce. This not only supports local economies but also ensures that the beers reflect the region's terroir, creating a sense of place in every sip. Seasonal beers, such as pumpkin ales in the fall or fresh hop IPAs in late summer, exemplify how brewers can highlight the uniqueness of their local ingredients.

Furthermore, the influence of global beer culture has opened the door to new styles. As craft brewers travel and explore different beer traditions from around the world, they often incorporate elements from those cultures into their brewing. From Japanese rice lagers to Mexican cervezas and Belgian-style sours, the blending of styles fosters a cross-cultural exchange that enriches the global beer landscape.

In conclusion, the future of beer is characterized by a spirit of innovation and experimentation. As brewers continue to challenge traditional brewing conventions and embrace new ingredients, techniques, and styles, the diversity of beer will only expand, inviting both seasoned enthusiasts and new drinkers to discover and enjoy an array of flavors that truly reflect the creativity and passion of modern brewing. This ongoing evolution not only enriches the beer experience but also emphasizes the role of beer as a dynamic cultural product that continues to adapt and thrive in a changing world.

Chapter 17

Beer Around the World

German Beer Culture: Reinheitsgebot and Traditions

Germany boasts one of the richest and most celebrated beer cultures in the world, characterized by a profound respect for tradition, quality, and the communal enjoyment of beer. Central to this culture is the Reinheitsgebot, or the German Beer Purity Law, which has shaped the brewing practices and standards in Germany since its inception in 1516. This law originally stipulated that only three ingredients—water, barley, and hops—could be used in the brewing of beer. Yeast was later included as a necessary fourth ingredient after its role in fermentation was understood.

The Reinheitsgebot: Historical Significance

The Reinheitsgebot was introduced in the Duchy of Bavaria by Duke Wilhelm IV as a measure to regulate brewing standards and protect consumers from adulterated and potentially harmful beverages. At a time when various substances were added to beer for flavoring and preservation, this law was revolutionary in establishing a baseline for purity and quality. The Reinheitsgebot not only safeguarded public health but also reinforced the cultural identity of Bavarian beer, which became synonymous with quality and craftsmanship.

Over the centuries, the Reinheitsgebot has become a point of national pride and a symbol of German brewing heritage. Although the European Union has since relaxed some of its restrictions, allowing for a wider variety of ingredients and brewing techniques, many German brewers still adhere to the principles of the Reinheitsgebot, viewing it as a commitment to quality and tradition.

Traditional Brewing Practices

German beer culture is deeply intertwined with traditional brewing practices that vary from region to region. The country is home to numerous beer styles, each with its own unique characteristics that reflect local ingredients, brewing methods, and historical influences. For example, the famous pilsner originates from the Czech Republic but has been embraced and adapted by German brewers, particularly in the regions of Bavaria and the north.

In Bavaria, the brewing tradition is particularly strong, exemplified by the annual Oktoberfest celebration in Munich. This festival, which began in 1810 as a royal wedding celebration, has evolved into the world's largest beer festival, drawing millions of visitors each year. It is a showcase of German beer culture, with traditional beer tents, folk music, and hearty Bavarian cuisine, all enjoyed in a convivial atmosphere.

The Role of Beer in Social Life

In German culture, beer is more than just a beverage; it is a social lubricant that fosters camaraderie and community. Pubs (or "Biergarten") and beer halls are central to social gatherings, where friends and families come together to enjoy beer, food, and conversation. The concept of the "Biergarten" originated in Bavaria as open-air spaces where beer was served, allowing patrons to enjoy their drinks in a relaxed and communal environment. This tradition has spread across the globe, but its roots remain firmly planted in Germany.

Moreover, beer is often featured in cultural and religious celebrations, from Christmas markets to harvest festivals. The act of toasting with beer is common during celebrations, symbolizing goodwill and a shared experience among participants.

Craft Beer Movement

In recent years, the craft beer movement has gained traction in Germany, paralleling trends seen in other parts of the world. While traditional breweries continue to thrive, a new wave of microbreweries has emerged, experimenting with innovative styles and flavors while still honoring the country's brewing heritage. This fusion of tradition and modernity has invigorated the German beer scene, attracting a new generation of beer enthusiasts eager to explore beyond the classic styles.

In conclusion, German beer culture, anchored by the Reinheitsgebot and enriched by centuries of tradition, remains a cornerstone of social life and national identity. It reflects not only a commitment to quality and purity but also a celebration of community, heritage, and the joy of sharing a good beer with friends.

Belgian Beer: Abbeys, Trappists, and Lambics

Belgium is renowned for its rich and diverse brewing heritage, characterized by a unique blend of tradition and innovation. Among the many styles that this country has to offer, Trappist and Abbey beers, as well as Lambics, stand out due to their historical significance, distinctive brewing methods, and cultural implications.

Trappist Beers

Trappist beers are produced by Trappist monks within the walls of their monasteries, adhering to strict brewing regulations that uphold both quality and tradition. Only beers brewed in

Trappist monasteries that meet specific criteria can bear the "Authentic Trappist Product" label. Currently, there are 14 Trappist breweries in the world, six of which are located in Belgium: Westmalle, Westvleteren, Rochefort, Orval, Chimay, and La Trappe.

The production of Trappist beer is closely tied to the monastic life, emphasizing self-sufficiency and community support. The revenue generated from these breweries often funds the monastery's charitable activities and upkeep. Each Trappist brewery boasts its own unique recipes and brewing techniques, resulting in a variety of flavors and styles, from rich, dark ales like Rochefort to the light, fruity Orval. The brewing process typically involves a secondary fermentation in the bottle, which enhances the complexity of flavors and textures. The monks' commitment to quality and authenticity has made Trappist beers some of the most sought-after and revered in the world.

Abbey Beers

While Trappist beers are brewed within the confines of monasteries, Abbey beers are produced by commercial breweries that may not be directly affiliated with a religious institution. However, many Abbey beers emulate the style and brewing traditions of Trappist beers, often using similar ingredients and methods. This category includes beers from breweries like Leffe and Affligem, which have become synonymous with Belgian beer culture.

Abbey beers typically feature a wide range of styles, including Dubbel, Tripel, and Quadrupel, each reflecting variations in malt, hops, and fermentation processes. Dubbel is characterized by its dark color and malty sweetness, while Tripels are usually paler, stronger, and more complex, often with a fruity and spicy character. Quadrupels, on the other hand, are rich and full-bodied, showcasing deep flavors of caramel and dark fruit.

Lambics

Lambics represent another unique facet of Belgian beer culture, distinguished by their spontaneous fermentation process. Unlike traditional brewing methods that rely on cultivated yeast strains, Lambics are fermented with wild yeasts and bacteria naturally present in the environment, particularly in the Senne Valley region near Brussels. This method imparts a complex flavor profile characterized by tartness and funkiness, making Lambics an acquired taste for many.

Among the most famous styles of Lambic are Gueuze and Kriek. Gueuze is a blend of young and old Lambics that undergo a secondary fermentation in the bottle, resulting in a sparkling, dry beer with a rich, sour flavor. Kriek, on the other hand, is a fruit Lambic, traditionally brewed with sour cherries, which adds a delightful sweetness and vibrant color to the final product.

Lambics are often aged for extended periods, allowing their flavors to develop and mature. The traditional brewing of Lambics is a testament to the artisanal approach of Belgian brewers, who prioritize the use of local ingredients and time-honored techniques.

Cultural Significance

The significance of Trappist, Abbey, and Lambic beers extends beyond their unique brewing methods; they are deeply woven into the social fabric of Belgian culture. Beer is often enjoyed during communal gatherings, celebrated in festivals, and served as an accompaniment to traditional Belgian cuisine. The intricate flavors and variety of styles highlight the craftsmanship of Belgian brewers, who have elevated beer to an art form.

In summary, Belgian beers, particularly Trappist, Abbey, and Lambics, exemplify a rich brewing tradition that is both historic and vibrant. They reflect the deep-rooted cultural values of community, craftsmanship, and the celebration of life, making Belgium a cornerstone of the global beer landscape.

The British Pub: Ale, Bitter, and the Role of Beer in British Society

The British pub, an institution steeped in history and culture, has played a pivotal role in shaping social norms and community interactions in the UK. Often referred to as "public houses," these establishments have served as social hubs, places of refuge, and venues for communal gathering for centuries. At the heart of this tradition is beer, particularly ales and bitters, which have become synonymous with pub culture.

Historical Context

The origins of the British pub can be traced back to the Roman occupation of Britain when taverns began to emerge as places where travelers could rest and refresh themselves with food and drink. Over the centuries, these establishments evolved, and during the Middle Ages, alehouses became widespread, often run by women known as "brewsters." By the 16th century, the rise of the gin craze and subsequent regulations led to the establishment of more formal public houses, which began serving a broader array of beverages, including wines and spirits.

However, it was beer—specifically ales and bitters—that captured the hearts of the British populace. Ales, which are fermented with top-fermenting yeast, were traditionally brewed at home or in small local breweries. The introduction of hops in the brewing process during the late Middle Ages provided beer with a distinctive bitter flavor and improved its preservation, paving the way for the popularity of pale ales and bitters.

The Role of Ale and Bitter

In the British pub, ale and bitter are not just beverages; they represent a rich tapestry of local tradition and craftsmanship. Bitter, a style of pale ale characterized by its hoppy flavor, became particularly popular in the 19th century with the rise of the Industrial Revolution and the growth of commercial breweries. The emergence of iconic beer brands, such as Bass and Guinness, further solidified the role of these styles within British culture.

Pubs began to offer a variety of bitters, often labeled as "ordinary," "best," and "special," which indicated their strength and flavor profile. The tradition of "cask ale," which is unfiltered and served from a cask, gained traction, emphasizing the importance of freshness and local brewing practices. This not only supported local economies but also fostered a sense of community as patrons often visited their neighborhood pubs to enjoy these locally crafted beers.

Social Significance

The British pub is a space where social hierarchies dissolve, and individuals from various walks of life come together. It serves as a backdrop for significant life events, from casual meet-ups to engagements, birthdays, and even funerals. The concept of the "local," a pub frequented by regulars, fosters deep relationships, making it a cornerstone of local identity.

Moreover, pubs have historically been venues for political discourse, community meetings, and cultural gatherings. The role of beer in these settings cannot be understated; it acts as a social lubricant, encouraging conversation and camaraderie. The phrase "meeting for a pint" encapsulates the informal nature of these gatherings, where discussions range from everyday concerns to serious political issues.

The Modern Pub Experience

In contemporary British society, the pub remains a vital part of community life, evolving to meet changing tastes and demographics. Gastro-pubs, for instance, offer a refined dining experience alongside traditional ales, appealing to a broader audience. Additionally, the craft beer movement has led to an explosion of microbreweries and artisan brewers, adding diversity to the offerings available in pubs across the nation.

In conclusion, the British pub is more than just a place to drink; it is a cultural institution that embodies the social fabric of British life. Ale and bitter are integral to this experience, linking generations and communities through shared stories, laughter, and a profound sense of belonging. As society continues to change, the pub's role may evolve, but its significance as a communal space will endure, celebrating the rich heritage of beer in British culture.

American Craft Beer: The Evolution of a New Tradition

The craft beer movement in America is a vibrant and dynamic evolution that reflects the broader cultural shifts and values of society since the late 20th century. The roots of this movement can be traced back to a desire for authenticity, quality, and innovation, distinguishing it from the mass-produced lagers and ales that dominated the American beer landscape for much of the 20th century.

In the early 1960s, the American beer market was largely monopolized by a handful of large brewing companies that produced light lagers, such as Budweiser, Miller, and Coors. This lack of diversity in beer styles and flavors left many beer enthusiasts yearning for something more flavorful and unique. The seeds of the craft beer revolution were planted when pioneers like Fritz Maytag of Anchor Brewing in San Francisco began to experiment with traditional brewing methods, introducing richer, more complex ales that harkened back to European brewing traditions.

The formal establishment of the craft beer movement is often marked by the 1980s, when the American Homebrewers Association was founded in 1978, coinciding with the legalization of homebrewing in the United States. This change empowered amateur brewers to explore their creativity and craft unique beers, sparking a newfound interest in brewing among the general public. By the end of the decade, the first wave of microbreweries began to emerge, with establishments like Sierra Nevada Brewing Co. and Samuel Adams leading the charge.

As the 1990s progressed, the craft beer movement gained momentum and visibility, catalyzing a cultural shift toward appreciating local, artisanal products. The Brewers Association, formed in 2005, played a pivotal role in promoting and supporting small, independent breweries. By 2000, there were over 1,500 craft breweries in the United States, a number that skyrocketed to over 8,000 by 2019, demonstrating the movement's explosive growth and widespread appeal.

One of the defining characteristics of American craft beer is its emphasis on creativity and experimentation. Craft brewers are known for pushing the boundaries of traditional beer styles, often incorporating unconventional ingredients such as fruits, spices, and even culinary elements like coffee and chocolate. This innovative spirit has given rise to a plethora of distinct beer styles, from hop-forward India Pale Ales (IPAs) to rich stouts and sour ales. The desire for experimentation has not only led to new flavor profiles but has also fostered a sense of community among breweries, many of which collaborate on special brews, sharing techniques and knowledge in a spirit of camaraderie.

The rise of craft beer has also been accompanied by a growing awareness of sustainability and social responsibility within the brewing industry. Many craft breweries prioritize eco-friendly practices, sourcing local ingredients, reducing waste, and engaging in community initiatives. This commitment to sustainability resonates with consumers who are increasingly valuing ethical and environmentally conscious choices in their purchasing decisions.

The craft beer movement has significantly influenced American culture, transforming beer from a mere commodity into a symbol of identity and community. Craft breweries have become social hubs, hosting events, tastings, and festivals that celebrate beer culture. The proliferation of craft beer bars and taprooms has created spaces where enthusiasts can gather, share experiences, and foster connections, reinforcing the notion of beer as a social lubricant.

In conclusion, the evolution of American craft beer represents a rich tapestry of creativity, community, and cultural identity. From its humble beginnings in homebrewing to the establishment of thousands of independent breweries, the craft beer movement has not only diversified the American beer landscape but has also challenged traditional notions of beer consumption, making it an integral part of modern American society. The future of craft beer looks promising as brewers continue to innovate and inspire, ensuring that this new tradition remains vibrant and influential for generations to come.

Beer in Asia: The Rise of Craft Breweries in China and Japan

In recent years, the beer landscape in Asia has undergone a significant transformation, particularly in China and Japan, where traditional brewing practices are giving way to a burgeoning craft beer movement. This shift reflects not only changing consumer preferences but also a broader cultural evolution in how beer is perceived and enjoyed.

The Chinese Craft Beer Revolution

China, once primarily known for its mass-produced lagers like Tsingtao and Snow Beer, has experienced a craft beer renaissance over the past decade. The rise of craft breweries in urban centers such as Beijing, Shanghai, and Shenzhen has been fueled by a younger generation of beer drinkers seeking variety and quality over quantity. The craft beer scene in China is marked by innovation, with brewers experimenting with local ingredients, flavors, and brewing techniques.

One of the key drivers of this movement is the increasing interest in artisanal products and a growing middle class willing to pay a premium for unique and high-quality beers. Microbreweries, often characterized by small-scale production and a focus on community engagement, have emerged as popular spots for socializing. They often feature a rotating selection of seasonal brews that highlight local and regional flavors, such as jasmine, Sichuan peppercorns, and even Chinese tea.

Additionally, the craft beer movement has been supported by the loosening of regulatory frameworks that previously stifled smaller producers. As the government recognizes the economic potential of craft brewing, more entrepreneurs are entering the market, resulting in a diverse range of styles from IPAs to stouts, often incorporating traditional Chinese ingredients.

Japanese Craft Beer: Tradition Meets Innovation

Japan's craft beer scene similarly reflects a blend of tradition and modernity. While Japan has a long history of brewing, dominated by major players like Asahi and Kirin, the craft beer movement began to gain traction in the 1990s with the introduction of the "Beer Act," which allowed smaller breweries to operate legally. This led to a surge in microbreweries, particularly in regions like Hokkaido, Kyoto, and Tokyo.

Japanese craft brewers are known for their meticulous attention to detail and a deep respect for the brewing process. They often draw inspiration from traditional Japanese brewing methods, such as those used in sake production, and incorporate local ingredients like rice, barley, and unique hops. This fusion of techniques and flavors has resulted in distinctive beer styles that reflect Japan's rich culinary heritage. For example, brewers have created innovative beers infused with yuzu, a citrus fruit native to East Asia, or matcha, green tea powder.

The craft beer culture in Japan is also characterized by an emphasis on community and sustainability. Many breweries focus on creating a local identity, often establishing taprooms that serve as social hubs for beer enthusiasts. The growing trend of "izakayas" (Japanese pubs) featuring craft beer has popularized the idea of pairing artisanal brews with traditional Japanese cuisine, creating a unique dining experience.

The Future of Craft Beer in Asia

The rise of craft breweries in China and Japan signals a broader shift in the beer market across Asia. As consumers increasingly seek diverse and high-quality options, the craft beer movement is likely to continue growing. This trend is not only transforming local beer cultures but also creating opportunities for international collaboration and exchange.

Moreover, the craft beer movement in these countries highlights the importance of local identity in brewing, encouraging brewers to experiment with ingredients that reflect their cultural heritage. As more people become interested in craft beer, the potential for innovation and growth in this sector remains high, promising an exciting future for beer enthusiasts in Asia and beyond.

Chapter 18

Beer and Gender

Women and Beer: From Ancient Brewsters to Modern Brewers

The history of beer is not only a chronicle of fermentation and flavor but also a narrative deeply intertwined with gender, particularly the influential role women have played throughout the ages. From the earliest days of brewing, women often occupied the position of brewsters, responsible for crafting this essential beverage in various cultures across the globe. Their contributions laid the groundwork for modern brewing practices, and their legacy continues to evolve in contemporary beer culture.

Ancient Brewsters

The origins of beer can be traced back to ancient civilizations, where women were commonly the primary brewers. In Mesopotamia, specifically among the Sumerians, archaeological evidence suggests that women brewed beer in their homes for both family consumption and larger social gatherings. This role was not merely domestic; beer was a significant part of Sumerian culture, often associated with rituals and celebrations. Women were celebrated as goddesses of brewing, such as Ninkasi, who was revered in hymns and mythology as the goddess of beer.

Similarly, in ancient Egypt, women played a crucial role in beer production, which was integral to daily life and religious practices. Beer was consumed by people of all ages and social classes, and it was often considered safer than water. Women brewed beer for their families and for commercial purposes, operating in both public and private spheres. The brewing process was typically a communal activity, further emphasizing the social nature of beer consumption.

The Middle Ages and Beyond

As societies evolved, so did the perception of women in brewing. During the Middle Ages, the advent of monasteries led to the professionalization of brewing. Monks became the predominant figures in beer production, overshadowing the historical prominence of women brewers. Despite this shift, women continued to brew beer in their homes and contribute to local economies. In many European towns, women were often the licensed brewers, a testament to their essential role in maintaining the brewing tradition.

The commercialization of beer in the Renaissance period saw the rise of commercial breweries, which were often male-dominated. However, women remained involved in various capacities, including as tavern keepers and pub owners. They managed establishments where beer was sold and served, thus continuing to influence beer culture and commerce.

The Modern Era
The 20th century marked a significant turning point for women in the brewing industry. While the Prohibition era in the United States forced many breweries to close, it also provided women with opportunities to enter the workforce and take on roles that were previously limited to men. After the repeal of Prohibition, however, the brewing industry faced significant challenges, and women's contributions were often overlooked.

The craft beer movement of the late 20th and early 21st centuries heralded a renaissance for women in brewing. With the rise of microbreweries and brewpubs, women found new avenues to express their creativity and expertise. Today, women are reclaiming their historical roles as brewers, with many leading successful breweries and innovating within the industry. Organizations like the Pink Boots Society and the Brewers Association's Women in Brewing initiative have been pivotal in supporting women in the craft beer community, providing networking, scholarships, and education opportunities.

Moreover, the modern craft beer scene has witnessed a shift in marketing and branding, with many breweries embracing gender-neutral approaches. The rise of women-led breweries has also inspired a new generation of beer enthusiasts who appreciate diversity in brewing and flavor.

Conclusion
From ancient brewsters to modern brewers, women have played an essential role in the history and culture of beer. Their contributions have shaped the brewing landscape, influencing not only the production of beer but also the social dynamics surrounding its consumption. As we celebrate the rich heritage of beer, it is vital to recognize and honor the women who have contributed to this storied beverage, ensuring that their legacy is acknowledged and continued in the present and future of brewing.

Gendered Marketing in the Beer Industry: Breaking Stereotypes
The beer industry has long been characterized by a male-centric image, perpetuated through marketing strategies that often reinforce traditional gender norms. Historically, beer advertising has targeted men, promoting notions of masculinity associated with strength, power, and dominance. This approach not only marginalizes women as consumers but also shapes societal perceptions of beer as a "male drink." However, there has been a notable shift in

the industry, with many brands beginning to challenge these stereotypes and adopt more inclusive marketing practices.

One of the key factors driving this change is the growing recognition of women as significant consumers of beer. Research indicates that women are not only increasingly participating in beer consumption but are also influential in the purchasing decisions within households. Brands have started to realize that appealing to a broader audience can expand their market share and build customer loyalty. This has led to a transformation in marketing strategies, as companies seek to create campaigns that resonate with diverse demographics.

Several breweries have taken creative steps to redefine their branding and challenge gender stereotypes. For instance, brands like BrewDog have launched campaigns specifically designed to appeal to women, using messaging that emphasizes empowerment and independence. Their "Equal Pay" campaign, which aimed to raise awareness about gender pay gaps, showcased women as strong and capable individuals rather than just passive consumers. Such initiatives not only attract female customers but also enhance brand reputation and social responsibility.

Moreover, the rise of craft breweries has played a pivotal role in this shift. Many craft brewers are founded by women or are committed to creating inclusive environments that welcome all beer enthusiasts. These breweries often focus on storytelling and community engagement, showcasing diverse voices and experiences in their marketing. By highlighting female brewers and featuring women in promotional materials, they challenge the traditional narrative that beer is exclusively for men.

In addition to changing their marketing narratives, some companies have also begun to reconsider the imagery used in their advertising. Gone are the days of scantily clad women in commercials designed to capture male attention. Brands are now opting for representations that celebrate diversity and authenticity, showcasing women enjoying beer in everyday settings, thereby normalizing female beer consumption. This approach not only enriches the brand image but also fosters a sense of belonging among female consumers, who can see themselves reflected in the marketing.

The impact of gendered marketing extends beyond consumer behavior; it also influences the brewing culture itself. As more women enter the brewing profession, from homebrewers to industry leaders, the narrative surrounding beer is evolving. This shift is evident in the increasing number of women-led breweries and initiatives aimed at supporting women in brewing. Organizations like the Pink Boots Society, which focuses on empowering women in the beer industry through education and networking, are gaining prominence, further encouraging female participation and visibility in the sector.

Despite these advancements, challenges remain. The beer industry still grapples with deeply ingrained stereotypes, and some consumers may resist the shift towards inclusivity. However, as societal norms continue to evolve and the demand for authentic representation grows, brands that embrace diversity in their marketing strategies are likely to thrive.

In conclusion, breaking gender stereotypes in beer marketing is crucial not only for the industry's growth but also for fostering a more inclusive society. As brands continue to adapt and innovate, they have the opportunity to reshape perceptions of beer and create a culture that values all consumers, regardless of gender. By challenging traditional norms and embracing diversity, the beer industry can set a precedent for other sectors, paving the way for a more equitable landscape.

The Rise of Women-Led Breweries and Craft Beer Brands

In recent years, the craft beer movement has witnessed a significant shift towards inclusivity and diversity, with women taking on increasingly prominent roles in the brewing industry. This rise of women-led breweries and craft beer brands not only reflects changing societal norms but also brings fresh perspectives and innovative ideas to a traditionally male-dominated field.

Historically, women have played crucial roles in brewing, dating back to ancient civilizations where they were often responsible for the production of beer. In Mesopotamia, for instance, women were recognized as brewers and even held positions of respect within their communities. However, as the brewing industry evolved, especially during the Industrial Revolution, the participation of women diminished, and brewing became largely associated with men. This trend persisted throughout the 20th century, culminating in a craft beer landscape that was predominantly male.

The resurgence of interest in craft brewing in the late 20th century sparked a new wave of creativity and entrepreneurship. As women began to reclaim their historical roles in brewing, they started establishing their own breweries and craft beer brands. The shift was not merely about gender representation; it was about infusing the industry with diverse flavors, styles, and business approaches that resonate with a broader audience.

One of the pioneers in this movement is Garrett Oliver, the brewmaster of Brooklyn Brewery, who has spoken extensively on the importance of diversity in brewing. His advocacy has encouraged women to step into leadership roles, and many have responded. Breweries such as

Sierra Nevada and Brooklyn Brewery have made concerted efforts to support and promote women in brewing through mentorship programs and scholarships.

Women-led breweries have emerged across the globe, each bringing unique narratives and brewing philosophies. For instance, Erdinger Brewery in Germany, one of the largest wheat beer producers, is operated by a woman who emphasizes traditional brewing methods while innovating with new recipes. In the United States, Elysian Brewing Company co-founders Dale and Dick Cantwell were among the first to recognize the significance of female brewers, hiring women in key positions and promoting a culture of inclusivity.

Craft beer brands led by women often prioritize community engagement and sustainability, reflecting a holistic approach to brewing. For example, The Pink Boots Society, founded by women in the brewing industry, aims to assist women in advancing their careers through education and networking opportunities. Their initiatives include scholarships for women seeking to enhance their brewing skills, fostering a supportive environment for those looking to break into the industry.

Furthermore, the marketing strategies of women-led breweries often challenge traditional gender norms. Many female brewers are focused on creating beers that appeal to a broader demographic, breaking away from the archetypal images associated with beer consumption. They emphasize storytelling, authenticity, and community involvement, thereby attracting a diverse clientele that includes women and younger consumers who may not have previously identified with beer culture.

As the craft beer movement continues to grow, the contributions of women-led breweries and craft beer brands are becoming increasingly significant. They are not only reshaping the industry landscape but also inspiring a new generation of brewers. The rise of these women-led initiatives is a testament to the transformative power of diversity in brewing, ensuring that the industry evolves and adapts to the tastes and values of a modern audience.

In conclusion, the rise of women-led breweries and craft beer brands is a pivotal development in the history of brewing. It not only acknowledges the historical contributions of women to beer production but also fosters innovation and inclusivity in the industry. As these women continue to break barriers and redefine brewing culture, they are paving the way for a more equitable and vibrant craft beer landscape.

The History of Beer as a Gender-Neutral Drink

The history of beer is deeply intertwined with human civilization, serving not only as a staple beverage but also as a social lubricant that transcends gender boundaries. Throughout history, beer has been consumed by a diverse array of people, irrespective of gender, and has played a significant role in social gatherings, rituals, and daily life. This inherent quality of beer as a gender-neutral drink can be traced back to ancient practices and continues to evolve in contemporary culture.

In ancient societies, beer was often produced and consumed by both men and women. The earliest evidence of beer-making can be found in Mesopotamia, where Sumerians brewed beer primarily from barley. Archaeological findings suggest that women were not only the primary brewers but also the main consumers of beer in these early civilizations. For instance, the Sumerian goddess Ninkasi was celebrated as the deity of beer, and hymns dedicated to her often included recipes for brewing. This indicates that beer held a central place in both domestic life and religious practices, uniting people in shared rituals that crossed gender lines.

As civilizations evolved, beer maintained its status as a communal drink. In ancient Egypt, beer was a vital part of daily life for all social classes, serving as a source of nutrition and hydration. Women were involved in brewing and selling beer, and it was common for both men and women to partake in local beer gardens and taverns. The social aspect of beer consumption fostered camaraderie and inclusivity, making it an integral part of celebrations and gatherings that welcomed everyone, regardless of gender.

The medieval period saw a shift in brewing practices as monasteries began to play a significant role in beer production. Monks brewed beer not only for sustenance but also for trade and profit. Although brewing became more formalized and associated with male-dominated institutions, the consumption of beer remained a gender-neutral activity. Taverns and alehouses served as social hubs where both men and women gathered to drink, share stories, and conduct business. The convivial atmosphere of these establishments reinforced the idea of beer as a unifying force, fostering community among diverse groups.

The Industrial Revolution brought profound changes to beer production and consumption, with the rise of commercial breweries and mass production. As beer became more accessible, it solidified its position as a drink enjoyed by all. The advent of lager in the 19th century, particularly in the United States, further popularized beer across different demographics. Saloon culture in America allowed women to enter public spaces where beer was served, challenging prevailing social norms and expectations about gender roles.

In contemporary society, the perception of beer as a gender-neutral drink continues to flourish, despite lingering stereotypes that associate beer consumption predominantly with men. The craft beer movement has played a pivotal role in reshaping this narrative, with many breweries actively promoting inclusivity. Women have emerged as influential figures in the craft beer industry, from brewers and owners to beer judges and festival organizers. Their contributions have helped to dismantle outdated stereotypes and demonstrate that beer is a beverage for everyone.

Beer festivals and events increasingly embrace diversity, showcasing the creativity and innovation of women in brewing. Initiatives aimed at empowering women in the beer industry have gained traction, reinforcing the concept of beer as a drink that transcends gender. As society continues to evolve, the history of beer as a gender-neutral drink serves as a testament to its ability to unite people across different backgrounds and experiences, celebrating the joy of communal consumption and shared traditions.

In conclusion, beer's journey through history illustrates its role as a gender-neutral drink, fostering inclusivity and community. From ancient times to the present day, beer has proven to be a beverage that transcends gender divisions, inviting all to partake in its rich cultural heritage.

Women in Beer Festivals and Competitions

The landscape of the beer industry has evolved dramatically over the years, with women increasingly taking center stage in beer festivals and competitions. Historically, brewing was predominantly a male-dominated field, but recent trends have demonstrated a significant shift. Today, women are not only participating in these events but are also excelling and making substantial contributions to the culture and craft of brewing.

Historical Context

In ancient times, women were often the primary brewers in their households. Societies such as the Sumerians and Egyptians recognized the role of women in brewing, where they prepared beer for everyday consumption and ceremonial purposes. However, as brewing transitioned into a commercial industry during the Middle Ages and beyond, the craft became increasingly male-oriented. The Industrial Revolution further cemented this trend, leading to a decline in women's roles in brewing.

Yet, as the craft beer movement gained momentum in the late 20th century, women began to reclaim their place in the brewing community. Organizations such as the Pink Boots Society, formed in 2007, have actively worked to support women in the brewing industry through scholarships, mentorship, and networking opportunities.

Participation in Festivals

Beer festivals have become a vibrant celebration of brewing culture, often showcasing local and international brews, and providing platforms for breweries of all sizes. Women are now integral to these festivals, both as participants and organizers. Events like the Great American Beer Festival and the World Beer Cup feature categories specifically recognizing women's contributions, celebrating female brewers, and highlighting beers crafted by women-led breweries.

Women-led breweries are gaining recognition, and their presence at festivals has become more prominent. These breweries often bring unique perspectives and flavors to the craft, challenging traditional brewing norms. Female brewers frequently use innovative ingredients or brewing techniques that reflect their diverse backgrounds and experiences, enriching the overall beer landscape.

Competitions and Recognition

Competitions have also seen a notable increase in female participation. Many beer competitions now have categories or awards specifically dedicated to recognizing the achievements of women brewers. Additionally, women are often included in judging panels, bringing a fresh perspective to the evaluation process and promoting diversity within the judging criteria.

One notable example is the Women's Beer Competition, which aims to showcase beers produced by female brewers while also encouraging women to enter the brewing profession. Such competitions not only recognize the quality of beers crafted by women but also serve as a platform for networking and mentorship among aspiring female brewers.

Cultural Shifts

The growing presence of women in beer festivals and competitions signifies a cultural shift within the beer community. Events are increasingly focused on inclusivity and diversity, with organizers actively seeking to engage women, people of color, and other underrepresented groups. This shift has fostered a more collaborative environment, where knowledge-sharing and innovation thrive.

Moreover, women are utilizing beer festivals as a means to address broader social issues, such as sustainability and community engagement. Many female brewers are committed to eco-friendly practices and social responsibility, using their platforms at festivals to educate attendees about these important topics.

Conclusion

The participation of women in beer festivals and competitions marks a significant and positive trend in the brewing industry. As female brewers continue to break barriers and gain recognition, they inspire future generations to join the craft. With a growing emphasis on diversity, community, and innovation, women are not only reshaping the narrative around beer but are also contributing to a richer, more inclusive brewing culture. As the industry continues to evolve, the role of women will undoubtedly become even more pronounced, ensuring that their voices and talents remain an essential part of the global beer story.

Chapter 19

Beer and Sustainability

Reducing Waste in Brewing: Eco-Friendly Practices

Brewing beer is a complex process that generates a significant amount of waste, from spent grains to excess water. However, the brewing industry has increasingly recognized the importance of sustainability and has adopted several eco-friendly practices aimed at waste reduction. This not only benefits the environment but also enhances the overall efficiency and profitability of breweries.

Spent Grains Recycling

One of the most substantial byproducts of the brewing process is spent grains, which can account for up to 85% of the total solid waste generated. Traditionally, these grains were disposed of, leading to environmental concerns regarding landfill use. Today, many breweries are finding innovative ways to recycle spent grains.

Many breweries partner with local farms, donating spent grains as animal feed. This not only provides livestock with a nutritious food source but also reduces the need for additional feed production, which can be resource-intensive. Moreover, some breweries have explored the production of biofuels from spent grains, further diversifying their waste management strategies and contributing to renewable energy sources.

Water Conservation

Water is a critical ingredient in brewing, but it is also one of the most significant resources consumed in the process. The brewing cycle can use anywhere from 3 to 10 gallons of water for every gallon of beer produced. Recognizing this, many breweries are implementing water conservation measures.

This includes the installation of water-efficient systems, such as low-flow fixtures and water recycling systems. Some breweries have made substantial investments in treatment facilities that allow them to reuse wastewater for cleaning and other non-potable purposes. By recycling water, breweries not only minimize their environmental impact but also significantly cut down on water costs.

Energy Efficiency
Brewing is an energy-intensive process, requiring substantial heat and electricity. To reduce energy waste, many breweries are investing in energy-efficient technologies. For example, the use of heat recovery systems allows breweries to capture and reuse heat generated during the brewing process, significantly lowering energy consumption.

In addition, some breweries are exploring renewable energy options, such as solar panels and wind turbines, to power their operations. By reducing their reliance on fossil fuels, these breweries can lower their carbon footprint and contribute to a more sustainable energy landscape.

Sustainable Packaging
Packaging is another significant area where breweries are focusing their sustainability efforts. Traditional glass bottles are heavy and resource-intensive to produce, leading to higher emissions during transportation. Many breweries are now opting for lighter-weight bottles, cans, or even kegging systems that minimize packaging waste.

Additionally, some breweries are adopting eco-friendly materials, such as recyclable or biodegradable packaging, to reduce their impact on landfills. Innovative solutions, such as edible six-pack rings made from seaweed, are also emerging in the industry, showcasing creative approaches to sustainable packaging.

Education and Community Involvement
Beyond internal practices, many breweries are actively engaging their communities in sustainability efforts. This includes educational programs aimed at raising awareness about waste reduction and environmental responsibility. By hosting workshops, brewery tours, and community events, breweries can foster a culture of sustainability among consumers and local businesses.

In conclusion, reducing waste in brewing through eco-friendly practices is a crucial step towards a more sustainable industry. From recycling spent grains and conserving water to implementing energy-efficient systems and adopting sustainable packaging, breweries are leading the way in environmental stewardship. These efforts not only mitigate the ecological footprint of beer production but also promote a culture of sustainability that resonates with consumers and inspires future generations of brewers to prioritize eco-friendly practices. As the craft beer movement continues to grow, the commitment to reducing waste and embracing sustainability will be vital in shaping the future of brewing.

The Rise of Organic and Biodynamic Beer

The craft beer movement has revolutionized the brewing landscape, introducing a myriad of innovative styles and approaches to production. Among these, organic and biodynamic beers have gained significant traction in recent years, appealing to environmentally conscious consumers and enthusiasts seeking authenticity in their drinking experiences. This section delves into the rise of organic and biodynamic beer, exploring their definitions, production practices, and their impact on the broader beer industry.

Defining Organic and Biodynamic Beer

Organic beer is brewed using ingredients that are certified organic, meaning they are grown without synthetic pesticides, herbicides, or fertilizers. The certification process is regulated by government bodies in various countries, ensuring that the ingredients meet specific organic standards throughout their production lifecycle. In contrast, biodynamic beer goes a step further by incorporating principles of biodynamic agriculture, which is a holistic and sustainable farming approach developed by Rudolf Steiner in the early 20th century. Biodynamic farming emphasizes biodiversity, soil health, and the use of organic compost and preparations, often aligning with lunar cycles and cosmic rhythms for planting and harvesting.

Production Practices

The production of organic and biodynamic beer begins with the selection of ingredients. Organic barley, hops, and yeast are essential, and many breweries go beyond mere compliance, sourcing their ingredients from local organic farms. This not only supports local economies but also reduces the carbon footprint associated with transportation.

Water management is another critical aspect of organic brewing. Organic brewers often emphasize sustainable water usage, employing methods such as rainwater harvesting and advanced filtration systems to minimize waste. Additionally, the fermentation process may use wild yeast strains or specifically cultivated organic yeast, contributing unique flavors and characteristics to the final product.

Biodynamic brewers are particularly focused on the health of the entire ecosystem in which they operate. This includes crop rotation, the use of cover crops, and the integration of livestock to promote biodiversity and soil fertility. These practices not only ensure high-quality ingredients but also foster a connection between the brewer, the land, and the community.

The Market Demand

The rise of organic and biodynamic beer can be attributed to the growing consumer demand for products that are not only tasty but also environmentally sustainable and socially responsible.

As awareness of environmental issues grows, many consumers are seeking out products that align with their values. Studies have shown that consumers are willing to pay a premium for organic and biodynamic products, seeing them as healthier and more ethical choices.

Moreover, the craft beer community has embraced these practices as part of a broader movement towards sustainability and transparency. Many breweries proudly display their organic certifications, and beer festivals increasingly feature organic and biodynamic options, showcasing the diverse range of flavors and styles that can emerge from these practices.

Challenges and Future Outlook
While the rise of organic and biodynamic beer is promising, it is not without its challenges. The costs associated with organic farming and certification can be prohibitive, particularly for small-scale brewers. Additionally, the availability of organic ingredients can fluctuate, leading to potential supply chain issues.

Despite these challenges, the future of organic and biodynamic beer appears bright. As technology advances, more efficient and sustainable farming practices are being developed, making it easier for brewers to adopt organic methods. Furthermore, consumer interest in health, sustainability, and ethical consumption is likely to drive continued growth in this sector.

In conclusion, the rise of organic and biodynamic beer represents a significant shift in the brewing industry, reflecting broader societal trends towards sustainability and environmental consciousness. As consumers become increasingly aware of the impact of their choices, the demand for organic and biodynamic options is expected to grow, encouraging more brewers to embrace these practices and contribute to a more sustainable future for beer production.

Water Conservation in Brewing: A Growing Concern
Water is often referred to as the lifeblood of brewing. It is not only the primary ingredient in beer but also a critical component in various stages of the brewing process—from mashing the grains to cleaning equipment. However, as the brewing industry continues to expand globally, the challenge of water conservation has emerged as a significant concern. This is particularly pressing in light of climate change, population growth, and increasing water scarcity in many regions.

The brewing process typically requires a substantial amount of water. On average, it takes approximately four to six liters of water to produce one liter of beer, a figure that can vary based on the efficiency of the brewing system and the style of beer being produced. Traditional brewing practices, alongside the rising demand for craft beers, have led to concerns about the sustainability of water resources. As such, modern breweries are increasingly recognizing the need to adopt water conservation measures to reduce their environmental footprint and ensure the long-term viability of their operations.

One of the most effective strategies for water conservation in brewing is the implementation of water recycling and reuse systems. Many breweries have begun to invest in technologies that allow them to treat and reuse wastewater from the brewing process. This not only minimizes the amount of fresh water required but also reduces the volume of wastewater released into local water systems. For instance, some breweries recycle water used in cooling processes, cleaning tanks, and even in the brewing itself. By repurposing water, these facilities can significantly lower their overall consumption and operational costs.

In addition to recycling, breweries are also focusing on optimizing their brewing processes to minimize water usage. This can involve the adoption of state-of-the-art brewing equipment that utilizes less water or the redesign of brewing recipes to require fewer water-intensive steps. For example, brewers are increasingly using dry-hopping techniques that reduce the need for water in the fermentation process. Furthermore, innovations in brewing technology, such as automated systems that precisely control water flow and temperature, can lead to more efficient operations overall.

Another essential aspect of water conservation in brewing is educating staff and fostering a culture of sustainability within the brewery. Employees play a vital role in identifying areas where water can be saved, whether during the brewing process, cleaning procedures, or maintenance of equipment. Training programs that highlight the importance of water conservation can lead to more mindful practices and greater accountability across the organization.

Collaboration and partnerships are also crucial in addressing water conservation challenges in the brewing industry. Many breweries are now working with local governments, environmental organizations, and other businesses to develop water conservation strategies and share best practices. These partnerships can lead to community-wide initiatives that benefit not only the breweries but also the local ecosystems and populations that depend on these water resources.

Finally, the growing consumer demand for sustainable practices is prompting breweries to take water conservation seriously. Many beer drinkers are increasingly conscious of the environmental impact of their choices, leading breweries to promote their water-saving efforts as part of their brand identity. This not only helps attract environmentally-minded consumers but also fosters a sense of community and shared responsibility in the pursuit of sustainable brewing practices.

In conclusion, water conservation is a growing concern in the brewing industry as the pressure to utilize resources responsibly intensifies. By implementing water recycling systems, optimizing brewing processes, fostering a culture of sustainability, collaborating with stakeholders, and responding to consumer demand, breweries can play a pivotal role in promoting water conservation. As the industry adapts to these challenges, it will not only ensure its own sustainability but also contribute positively to the environment and society at large.

Recycling Spent Grains: Innovations in Reusing Byproducts

Spent grains, the solid residue remaining after the mashing process in beer production, account for a significant byproduct of the brewing industry. Traditionally, these grains were often disposed of as waste, but recent innovations have transformed how breweries approach spent grain management, reflecting a growing commitment to sustainability and resource efficiency. This shift not only minimizes environmental impact but also opens up new avenues for economic opportunities within the brewing community.

The Composition and Value of Spent Grains

Spent grains are primarily composed of barley husks, endosperm, and other cereal grains that have already contributed their sugars and nutrients to the brewing process. Typically, a brewery can produce hundreds to thousands of pounds of spent grains per batch, depending on its scale. This byproduct is rich in protein, fiber, and essential nutrients, making it a valuable resource for various applications beyond beer production.

Sustainable Practices in Spent Grain Management

1. Animal Feed: One of the most common uses for spent grains is as animal feed, particularly for livestock. Many breweries have established partnerships with local farms, allowing them to donate spent grains, which can be used to supplement the diets of cattle, pigs, and poultry. This not only reduces waste but also lowers feed costs for farmers, creating a symbiotic relationship between the agricultural and brewing sectors.

2. Food Products: Innovative breweries have started to explore the potential of spent grains in food manufacturing. Brands have emerged that produce baked goods, granola bars, and snacks utilizing spent grains as a key ingredient. These products not only capitalize on the nutritional benefits of spent grains but also appeal to environmentally conscious consumers looking for sustainable food options.

3. Biogas Production: Another promising avenue is the conversion of spent grains into biogas through anaerobic digestion. This process allows the organic matter in spent grains to break down, producing methane gas that can be harnessed as a renewable energy source. Some breweries have successfully implemented biogas systems, generating energy that can be used to power their operations or be fed back into the grid, contributing to energy sustainability.

4. Mushroom Cultivation: Spent grains have also found a niche in the cultivation of gourmet mushrooms. Fungi thrive on the nutrient-rich organic material found in spent grains, and several entrepreneurial ventures have emerged that focus on recycling this byproduct into high-quality mushroom crops. This not only helps reduce waste but also creates a unique product that can be marketed alongside the brewery's offerings.

5. Crafting and Home Brewing: Home brewers and craft enthusiasts have begun to incorporate spent grains into their brewing and baking practices. Spent grain flour is gaining popularity in home kitchens for baking bread and other goods, allowing home brewers to make the most of their brewing experience while minimizing waste.

Challenges and Considerations

Despite the potential benefits of recycling spent grains, challenges remain. The timeliness of utilizing the byproduct is crucial, as spent grains have a limited shelf life and can spoil if not processed promptly. Additionally, regulatory considerations regarding food safety and animal feed standards must be adhered to, requiring breweries to navigate complex guidelines to ensure their practices are compliant.

Conclusion

The innovative reuse of spent grains is a testament to the brewing industry's commitment to sustainability and environmental responsibility. By repurposing this byproduct, breweries not only reduce waste but also create economic opportunities that benefit local communities. As the industry continues to evolve, the creative approaches to spent grain recycling will likely expand, further integrating sustainability into the fabric of brewing culture. This not only enhances the brewery's operational efficiency but also promotes a more circular economy, illustrating how even waste can be transformed into valuable resources.

Solar-Powered Breweries: Green Energy in Brewing

As the world grapples with the pressing challenges of climate change and environmental sustainability, industries across the globe are seeking innovative solutions to reduce their carbon footprints. The brewing industry, with its significant energy demands, has emerged as a key player in this green revolution. Among the various sustainable practices being adopted, solar-powered breweries stand out as a beacon of hope for a more environmentally conscious future.

The Energy Footprint of Brewing

Brewing beer is an energy-intensive process, involving heating, cooling, and the operation of various machinery. Traditional brewing methods often rely on fossil fuels, which contribute to greenhouse gas emissions. In response to growing environmental concerns, many breweries are reevaluating their energy sources and looking for ways to minimize their ecological impact. Utilizing renewable energy, primarily solar power, has become an attractive alternative due to its abundance and decreasing costs.

Harnessing Solar Power

Solar-powered breweries typically employ photovoltaic (PV) panels that convert sunlight into electricity. These installations can be integrated into the brewery's architecture, often placed on rooftops or designated solar farms nearby. The electricity generated can be used directly for brewing operations, lighting, and refrigeration, significantly reducing reliance on conventional power sources.

For instance, some breweries have reported achieving up to 100% of their energy needs through solar panels, particularly in sunny regions where solar energy is most effective. This shift not only helps to cut operational costs in the long run but also enhances a brewery's brand image as a sustainable and eco-friendly establishment.

Case Studies in Solar Brewing

Several breweries worldwide have successfully implemented solar energy solutions. One notable example is the Sierra Nevada Brewing Co. in California. With a robust commitment to sustainability, Sierra Nevada has installed a large solar array that produces approximately 1.5 million kilowatt-hours of energy annually. This initiative has significantly reduced the brewery's carbon emissions, demonstrating a commitment to environmental stewardship.

Similarly, Brooklyn Brewery in New York has taken steps toward sustainability by incorporating solar energy into their operations. While not entirely powered by solar, they have made strides to utilize renewable sources and educate their customers about the benefits of green brewing practices.

Benefits Beyond Energy Savings
The shift to solar energy in brewing extends beyond just cost savings and reduced emissions. It serves as a powerful marketing tool, appealing to environmentally conscious consumers who prefer to support businesses that prioritize sustainability. A brewery's commitment to solar power can attract a loyal customer base, as consumers increasingly seek brands that align with their values regarding environmental responsibility.

Furthermore, solar-powered breweries can inspire other local businesses, creating a ripple effect in the community. By showcasing the feasibility and benefits of solar energy, these breweries can encourage restaurants, bars, and other local enterprises to explore renewable energy options, ultimately fostering a collective effort toward sustainability.

Challenges and Future Directions
While the transition to solar energy presents numerous advantages, it is not without its challenges. Initial setup costs for solar installations can be substantial, and breweries need to navigate regulatory frameworks and incentives that vary by region. Additionally, the intermittent nature of solar energy requires a reliable backup system to ensure uninterrupted brewing processes.

Despite these hurdles, the future of solar-powered breweries looks promising. As technology advances and solar energy becomes increasingly accessible, more breweries are likely to adopt these eco-friendly practices. The integration of energy storage systems and smart grid technology could further enhance the viability of solar energy in brewing.

In conclusion, solar-powered breweries represent a significant step toward a sustainable future in the brewing industry. By embracing renewable energy, breweries not only reduce their environmental impact but also set a standard for responsible business practices. The continued growth of solar energy adoption in brewing could pave the way for a greener, more sustainable beer culture worldwide.

Chapter 20

The Role of Beer in Modern Society

Beer as a Social Lubricant: The Role of Beer in Social Gatherings

Beer has long been recognized as more than just a beverage; it serves as a social lubricant that fosters connections among individuals, igniting conversations and facilitating interactions across diverse settings. This phenomenon is rooted deeply in cultural traditions and social practices that span centuries, with beer playing a pivotal role in community bonding, celebration, and even negotiation.

The origins of beer as a catalyst for social interaction can be traced back to ancient civilizations, where communal drinking was often associated with religious rituals and social gatherings. In Mesopotamia, for instance, beer was consumed during festivals, signifying unity and collective enjoyment. Similarly, in ancient Egypt, beer was not only a staple in daily life but also an integral part of religious ceremonies and communal feasts. These early uses of beer established a foundation for its role as a facilitator of social cohesion.

In medieval Europe, the significance of beer continued to flourish within communities. Taverns and public houses became vital social spaces where people gathered to share stories, conduct business, and resolve disputes. The act of sharing a drink transformed strangers into acquaintances, fostering a sense of camaraderie. Such establishments were often hotspots for community events, from local elections to weddings. The social dynamics that emerged in these settings were underpinned by the relaxed atmosphere that beer provided, encouraging open dialogue and informal interactions.

In contemporary society, beer retains its status as a social lubricant, especially in social gatherings such as parties, barbecues, and festivals. The consumption of beer often acts as a bridge between individuals, breaking down barriers of social anxiety and facilitating connections. The ritual of toasting, for example, encapsulates the essence of shared experience, promoting goodwill and a sense of togetherness. Beer, in these contexts, becomes a means of celebrating milestones, from birthdays to promotions, enhancing the overall experience of the event.

Moreover, the rise of craft beer culture has further enriched the social landscape surrounding beer consumption. Microbreweries and brewpubs have emerged as community hubs where beer enthusiasts congregate to explore new flavors and styles, engage in tastings, and participate in brewing workshops. These environments foster a sense of belonging and shared passion, often leading to friendships that extend beyond the brewery's walls. The craft beer movement also emphasizes local production, which can deepen connections within communities, as individuals support local businesses while enjoying a product that reflects their cultural identity.

Beer festivals exemplify the power of beer as a social lubricant on a larger scale. These events celebrate not only beer but also the communities that brew it. Festivals bring together people from various backgrounds, united by a common appreciation for beer. The communal atmosphere encourages interaction, with attendees sharing experiences and recommendations, often resulting in new friendships and collaborations. These gatherings also provide a platform for cultural exchange, showcasing diverse brewing traditions and styles, thereby enriching the social fabric of the community.

Importantly, beer's role as a social lubricant is not without its complexities. While it can foster community and connection, there is also the potential for overconsumption and its associated risks. Responsible drinking remains essential in ensuring that beer continues to be a positive force in social interactions, emphasizing moderation and mindfulness in consumption.

Ultimately, the role of beer as a social lubricant is deeply embedded in human culture, transcending time and geography. As communities continue to evolve, so too will the ways in which beer is enjoyed, serving as a timeless medium for connection, celebration, and social engagement. Whether in a bustling pub or a quiet backyard gathering, the presence of beer often invites camaraderie, transforming mere acquaintances into friends and fostering a sense of belonging that resonates through shared experiences.

Beer and Identity

In recent decades, the craft beer movement has transformed not only the brewing industry but also the social landscape surrounding beer consumption. Craft beer enthusiasts have emerged as a distinct community united by a passion for quality, diversity, and the cultural significance of beer. This section explores how the craft beer movement has shaped identities, created communities, and fostered a sense of belonging among its aficionados.

At its core, the craft beer movement represents a rebellion against mass-produced, homogenized beer. Enthusiasts often pride themselves on their knowledge of diverse styles, brewing techniques, and the stories behind each beer. This quest for authenticity resonates deeply with consumers who seek to connect with their beverages on a personal level. The craft beer community encourages exploration and experimentation, allowing drinkers to develop a more nuanced palate. This journey of discovery is often shared among friends and fellow beer lovers, solidifying bonds and creating a shared identity that transcends geographic and cultural boundaries.

Local breweries have become cultural hubs, fostering community engagement and pride. Many craft breweries embrace the concept of place, incorporating local ingredients and traditions into their recipes. This localization not only enhances the unique flavor profiles of their beers but also strengthens community ties. Beer enthusiasts often refer to their favorite local breweries as "their own," feeling a sense of ownership and loyalty that aligns with their identity as community members. Events such as brewery tours, tastings, and festivals allow enthusiasts to interact with brewers, learn about the brewing process, and celebrate the local craft beer scene. This engagement fosters a sense of belonging and reinforces their identity as advocates for local businesses and artisans.

The rise of social media has exponentially amplified the craft beer community's visibility and connectivity. Platforms like Instagram, Facebook, and Twitter enable enthusiasts to share their beer experiences, discover new breweries, and engage in conversations about beer culture. The hashtag CraftBeer has become a rallying cry, uniting enthusiasts across the globe. Online forums and beer rating apps allow consumers to exchange opinions, recommend brews, and even participate in virtual tastings, further enhancing their sense of belonging to a larger community.

Moreover, the craft beer movement has democratized beer culture, encouraging inclusivity and diversity. As craft breweries continue to proliferate, they often seek to cater to a wider audience by creating beers that appeal to different tastes, dietary requirements, and cultural backgrounds. This inclusivity is reflected in the rise of women-led breweries and initiatives aimed at promoting underrepresented voices in brewing. Organizations such as the Pink Boots Society and the Brewer's Association's diversity initiatives foster environments where everyone, regardless of gender or background, can participate in the brewing community. As a result, the craft beer movement has become a platform for social change, empowering marginalized groups and reshaping perceptions of who can be a brewer or a beer enthusiast.

The identity of craft beer enthusiasts is also tied to the values of sustainability and ethical consumption. Many craft breweries prioritize eco-friendly practices, sourcing local ingredients, and minimizing waste. Enthusiasts often gravitate toward brands that align with their personal values, such as supporting environmental initiatives or engaging in fair trade practices. This connection between personal identity and consumption choices deepens the bond within the craft beer community, as members collectively advocate for sustainability in their beer choices.

In conclusion, the rise of craft beer has not only redefined the beverage itself but also created vibrant communities characterized by shared values, exploration, and inclusivity. Beer enthusiasts find identity within this community, forming connections that transcend mere consumption, celebrating the artistry of brewing, and advocating for local and sustainable practices. As the craft beer movement continues to evolve, its impact on social identity and community cohesion remains a powerful testament to the enduring cultural significance of beer.

Beer and the Economy: Its Contribution to Employment and GDP

Beer has long transcended its status as a mere beverage; it is a vital economic driver in many regions worldwide. The contribution of beer to employment and gross domestic product (GDP) is substantial, affecting various sectors from agriculture to retail and hospitality.

Employment in the Beer Industry

The beer industry provides millions of jobs globally, encompassing a wide range of roles. This includes direct employment in breweries, which can vary from small craft operations to large multinational corporations, as well as indirect jobs in agriculture (barley and hop farming), distribution, and retail. According to the Brewers Association, in the United States alone, the craft brewing sector supports over 1.5 million jobs, including positions in brewing, marketing, sales, and management.

Beyond the brewing sector, the hospitality industry relies heavily on beer. Bars, restaurants, and pubs employ thousands of people, often creating positions specifically related to beer service. From bartenders to sommeliers who specialize in beer pairing, the beer industry fosters diverse employment opportunities. Additionally, ancillary businesses such as packaging, transportation, and advertising also benefit, amplifying the employment impact even further.

Contribution to GDP

Beer significantly contributes to national and local economies, reflected in GDP figures. The brewing industry generates substantial revenue through taxation, direct sales, and economic activity associated with production. For instance, in the United States, the beer industry contributed over $328 billion to the economy in 2019, according to the Beer Institute. This figure encompasses production, distribution, retail sales, and the taxes collected by federal, state, and local governments.

Tax revenues from beer are particularly noteworthy. Governments at various levels levy excise taxes on beer production and sales, which fund public services and infrastructure. These taxes are a significant source of revenue; for example, the U.S. federal government collected nearly $3.5 billion in excise taxes from beer in 2020. This revenue stream underscores the beer industry's importance to government budgets and public funding initiatives.

Economic Multiplier Effect

The economic impact of beer extends beyond direct employment and revenue generation. The concept of the economic multiplier effect illustrates how initial spending in the beer industry stimulates further economic activity. When breweries, bars, and restaurants invest in their operations, they purchase ingredients, equipment, and services from local suppliers, thereby creating a ripple effect throughout the local economy.

For example, a brewery purchasing barley from a local farmer not only supports the farmer's business but also stimulates agricultural jobs, transportation, and processing sectors. Furthermore, employees in the beer industry typically spend their wages in the local economy, contributing to the retail sector, housing, and services.

Craft Beer and Local Economies

The craft beer movement has revitalized many local economies, particularly in areas that may have experienced economic decline. Microbreweries and brewpubs often source ingredients locally, promote local culture, and attract tourism, benefiting not only the breweries themselves but also surrounding businesses such as hotels, restaurants, and shops. Beer festivals and tasting events draw visitors, creating additional economic opportunities for local vendors and service providers.

In summary, the beer industry is a powerful economic engine, contributing significantly to employment and GDP across various sectors. Its multifaceted impact extends from direct job creation in brewing to broader economic stimulation through associated industries and local communities. As beer continues to evolve, so too will its role in shaping economies and fostering community development worldwide. The interplay between beer and the economy highlights the importance of this beverage beyond enjoyment, underscoring its significance in daily life and economic health.

The Role of Beer in Celebrations

Beer, one of humanity's oldest beverages, has woven itself into the fabric of societal celebrations across cultures and time. Its role in marking significant life events, such as weddings, holidays, and other special occasions, underscores its importance as a social lubricant and a symbol of communal joy and festivity.

Weddings: A Toast to Unity

In many cultures, beer plays a pivotal role in wedding celebrations. The act of toasting with beer symbolizes not only the union of two individuals but also the merging of families and communities. In traditional German weddings, for example, the couple often participates in a "beer barrel" ceremony, where they tap a keg together, signifying their commitment to support each other through life's challenges. This communal act invites friends and family to share in the joyous occasion, fostering a sense of belonging and support.

Moreover, craft breweries and local breweries increasingly cater to weddings, providing custom brews and personalized labels that reflect the couple's personality and story. Such offerings enhance the celebratory atmosphere and create lasting memories tied to the event. From signature beers to beer cocktails, the incorporation of beer into wedding receptions has become a trend that reflects a couple's unique tastes and values.

Holidays: A Global Tradition

Beer's role in holiday celebrations is a global phenomenon. Various cultures have specific beers or brewing traditions associated with their holidays. For instance, Oktoberfest in Germany is synonymous with large quantities of beer consumption, where millions gather to enjoy traditional brews in a festive atmosphere filled with music, dancing, and hearty food. This festival not only celebrates the harvest but also fosters a sense of community and cultural pride.

Similarly, in Mexico, the Day of the Dead (Día de los Muertos) often includes offerings of beer on altars for deceased loved ones. This gesture symbolizes the connection between the living and the dead, emphasizing the importance of shared moments, even in remembrance. Beer becomes a medium through which families celebrate their heritage and honor their ancestors.

In the United States, beer has become an integral part of many national holidays, such as Independence Day and Thanksgiving. Grilling in backyards, tailgating at sports events, and family gatherings often feature beer as a staple beverage, embodying the spirit of the occasion and enhancing the camaraderie among participants.

Special Occasions: A Beverage of Choice

Beyond weddings and holidays, beer also plays a significant role in various special occasions, from birthdays to milestones like graduations and retirements. In many cultures, sharing a beer signifies friendship and celebration, making it a favored choice for toasting achievements. The craft beer movement has further expanded the options available for these occasions, allowing individuals to choose unique brews that resonate with their personal experiences and preferences.

Beer festivals and tastings have also gained popularity as celebratory events, inviting beer enthusiasts to explore diverse flavors and styles in a convivial atmosphere. These festivals often celebrate local brewing traditions and foster community connections, creating a shared sense of joy and appreciation for the craft of brewing.

Conclusion

The role of beer in celebrations—whether at weddings, holidays, or special occasions—highlights its significance as a cultural artifact and social connector. It transcends mere consumption; it fosters connections, embodies traditions, and enhances the joy of human experiences. As societies continue to evolve, so too will the ways in which beer is integrated into life's milestones, ensuring that it remains a cherished beverage in the tapestry of celebration for generations to come.

Beer and Social Change: Charity and Philanthropy in the Beer Industry

The relationship between beer and social change is a rich tapestry woven from the threads of community engagement, philanthropy, and grassroots activism. The beer industry has historically served as both a social lubricant and a catalyst for positive societal transformation. Through charitable initiatives and philanthropic endeavors, breweries and their patrons have contributed to various causes, addressing local and global challenges.

Historical Context

From its inception, beer has played an integral role in community bonding. In ancient societies, it was often consumed in communal settings, fostering social cohesion. This tradition continues today, with breweries increasingly recognizing their role in supporting their communities. The onset of the craft beer movement in the late 20th century marked a significant shift; small, independent breweries began to embrace not just the production of unique and quality beers, but also a commitment to social responsibility.

Charitable Initiatives

Many breweries have established charitable programs that focus on a wide range of issues, including environmental sustainability, mental health awareness, education, and social justice. For example, some breweries donate a portion of their sales to local charities or initiate fundraising campaigns that align with their values.

One notable trend is the launch of special edition beers or events where proceeds are directed toward specific causes. For instance, breweries may create a limited-release beer to support disaster relief efforts, with all profits going to aid organizations. This not only raises funds but also helps raise awareness about important issues, fostering a culture of giving within the beer-drinking community.

Community Engagement
Breweries often serve as community hubs, hosting events that promote charitable causes. These can range from beer tastings and festivals to fun runs and community service days. Such events encourage participation from local residents, creating a sense of ownership over the initiatives. For example, many craft breweries have partnered with local nonprofits to organize charity events, where patrons can enjoy beer while contributing to meaningful causes. This approach not only aids in fundraising but also strengthens community bonds.

Supporting Social Justice
The beer industry has also become an arena for social justice advocacy. In recent years, a number of breweries have taken public stances on issues such as racial equity, LGBTQ+ rights, and gender equality. Some have implemented policies to create more inclusive workplaces, while others have actively supported movements like Black Lives Matter through donations and campaigns. This commitment to social justice reflects a growing awareness within the industry that it has both a platform and a responsibility to advocate for change.

The Rise of Women-Led Breweries
Women have historically played a significant role in brewing, often overlooked in mainstream narratives. However, the rise of women-led breweries and initiatives that promote gender equality in the industry has gained momentum. Many female brewers are not only creating exceptional beers but are also championing causes related to women's rights and empowerment. These breweries often engage in charitable activities that support women in their communities, highlighting the intersection of brewing and social change.

Conclusion
In summary, the beer industry has evolved into a powerful vehicle for charitable action and social change. Breweries, particularly those rooted in the craft movement, have embraced their roles as community leaders, employing their resources and platforms to support worthy causes and advocate for social justice. As consumers increasingly seek brands that align with their values, the commitment to philanthropy within the beer industry is likely to continue growing, further solidifying the relationship between beer and meaningful social impact. Through these efforts, the industry not only enriches the lives of those in the community but also transforms the perception of beer as merely a recreational beverage into a catalyst for positive change.

Printed in Great Britain
by Amazon